CITIES

Discover How They Work

with **25** PROJECTS

Kathleen M. Reilly

Illustrated by Tom Casteel

P9-ART-797

~ Latest titles in the *Build It Yourself* Series ~

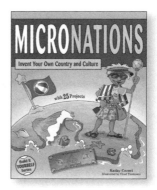
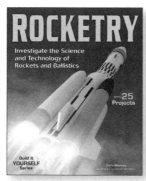
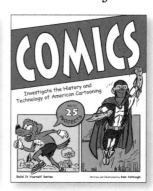

Nomad Press
A division of Nomad Communications
10 9 8 7 6 5 4 3 2 1

This book was manufactured by Sheridan Books, Ann Arbor, MI USA.
April 2014, Job #357565
ISBN: 978-1-61930-217-4

Illustrations by Tom Casteel
Educational Consultant, Marla Conn

Questions regarding the ordering of this book should be addressed to
Nomad Press
2456 Christian St.
White River Junction, VT 05001
www.nomadpress.net

Nomad Press is committed to preserving ancient forests and natural
resources. We elected to print *Cities: Discover How They Work* on
Thor PCW containing 30% post consumer waste.

Nomad Press made this paper choice because our printer, Sheridan Books, is a member of
Green Press Initiative, a nonprofit program dedicated to supporting authors, publishers,
and suppliers in their efforts to reduce their use of fiber obtained from endangered forests.

For more information, visit **www.greenpressinitiative.org**.

CONTENTS

8500–6500 BCE: Nomads (people without permanent homes) live off the land, following migrating animals and moving to areas with better conditions over the seasons.

4000–3500 BCE: Ancient people begin settling into groups, forming the first cities such as Ur in Mesopotamia.

1000 BCE: The first sanitation system is made in Burnt City, southeast of today's Iran.

312 BCE: The residents of Petra in Jordan build their homes directly into the walls of cliffs, instead of separate buildings like in today's cities.

300 CE: The Romans build and begin using 11 aqueducts to bring water into the city.

Words to know!

BCE: put after a date, BCE stands for Before Common Era and counts down to zero. CE stands for Common Era and counts up from zero. These non-religious terms correspond to BC and AD.

800 CE: In medieval Middle East, the first tar-paved roads are made near today's Baghdad in Iraq. The tar is made from petroleum from the oil fields in the region.

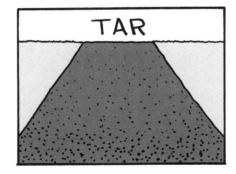

TAR

1664 CE: New York City's name is changed from New Amsterdam to New York when the English take over the area and the current King of England gives it to his brother, the Duke of York.

1804 CE: Philadelphia becomes the first city in the world to use cast iron pipes for water instead of wood. The city gives its old wooden pipes to Burlington, New Jersey—where they are used for another 80 years!

1863 CE: The first subway opens in London using gas-lit wooden carriages hauled by steam locomotives. In 1890, it becomes the first subway to use electric cars.

1880 CE: Wabash, Indiana, becomes the first city to have electric street lights. Although Wabash only has a population of 320, people come from miles around to witness the event. There are more than 10,000 people watching when the lights first come on!

1884 CE: The first skyscraper is built in Chicago. The Home Insurance Building is 10 stories tall—an amazing height for the times!

1912 CE: The first electric traffic light is created by Lester Wire, a policeman in Salt Lake City, Utah. It isn't actually installed until two years later, in Cleveland, Ohio.

2004 CE: Grand Haven, Michigan, becomes the first city with citywide wi-fi access. Six years later, there are 110 municipalities with citywide wi-fi available for public use.

2010 CE: The tallest skyscraper, Burj Khalifa, is built in Dubai. It is 2,722 feet (830 meters) tall.

2011 CE: On March 11, a massive earthquake and tsunami hits Tohohu, Japan. The most powerful known earthquake ever to hit Japan (and the fifth most powerful in the world since 1900), it destroys the city's infrastructure, causing extensive and severe structural damage.

2013 CE: A new law passes in France to reduce lighting at night. Window lighting in commercial buildings will be turned off after 1 a.m. This law is meant to reduce greenhouse gases and save energy.

Introduction

When you think of a "city," what comes to mind? If you live in a **suburban** or a **rural** area, you might imagine a city skyline with buildings of all sizes lined up against the horizon. Maybe you think of a city as an exciting place to visit. If you live in a city, you might picture your neighborhood grocery store or the two blocks you walk to your friend's house. It's home to you.

Words to know!

suburban: relating to an outlying district of a city.

rural: relating to the countryside rather than a city or town.

No matter what city you visit, you'll find a concentrated area with a large number of **residents**, activities, and businesses. These all work together and interact like big gears in a machine.

In a city you'll feel an energy that is very different from a rural area, which has large areas of open land where there aren't many houses or businesses. Open land might be owned by someone who doesn't want anything built on it, or it might be used as parkland or to raise **livestock**. Houses can be miles apart, and you have to take a "trip into town" in your car to go to stores and get supplies.

In between rural areas and cities are suburban areas with less open land. Houses are closer together, gathered in neighborhoods. You might be able to walk to a few stores, but usually you have to drive in your car.

In many cities, you almost never need to ride in a car. You can get most places by walking or taking **public transportation** such as a taxi, bus, or **subway**. You might live just steps away from your neighbors in an apartment or townhouse.

power grid: a network of cables above and below ground that carries electrical power throughout a region.

population: all of the people in an area or in a group.

EVERYTHING IN A CITY IS CLOSE BY.

In this book, you'll learn how cities started, how they've grown, and what their future looks like. You'll also get "up close" and discover how the many different and complex parts of a city work, such as the transportation system and the flow of water in, around, and out of the city. If you live in a city, you'll learn about the "hidden" parts of life around you that you don't think about in your daily life. For example, do you know how the **power grid** works? If you've never visited a city, you'll learn more about what's going on above and beneath ground than most people know who have lived there all their lives.

If you do get a chance to visit one of the many exciting cities of the world, you'll have a great appreciation for the planning, design, and operation involved in making sure all its systems are operating together. And you'll probably have more patience than the locals if the subway breaks down!

DID YOU KNOW?

According to the United Nations Population Fund, in 2008 there were about 3.3 billion people living in cities. This was the first time in history that the number of people living in cities exceeded the world's rural **population**. This number is expected to grow to 5 billion during the next 20 years.

CHAPTER 1

The Birth of a City

You wake up in the morning, climb out of bed, walk across the
room, and pull open the curtains of your apartment windows.
Outside, the world around you is already bustling and full of life.
Buses rumble past, bright yellow taxis honk their horns and pick up
passengers, customers hurry in and out of the stores carrying bags.
Dozens of people walk past on the sidewalk below. Streetlights blink
their directions to drivers and **pedestrians**, and there's a steady
stream of **urban** sounds. This is city life, and you're a part of it.

ALL THESE PEOPLE, ALL THIS ACTIVITY AND ORGANIZATION—IT WASN'T ALWAYS LIKE THIS. SO HOW DID CITIES START?

IN THE BEGINNING

Your distant ancestors didn't even have a permanent place to live. Around 8500–6500 BCE, **nomads** moved around, following the **migration** patterns of the animals they hunted for food and the growing seasons of the plants they ate.

Over time, people figured out how to settle in certain areas. They learned to grow **crops** and to raise animals for food. Groups of people settled together for safety, companionship, and to share the work. These were the first permanent **communities**—the earliest beginnings of the cities we know today.

Words to know!

pedestrian: someone traveling on foot.

urban: relating to a city or large town.

nomad: a person who moves from place to place in search of food.

migration: the movement of a large group of animals or people from one location to another.

crop: a plant grown for food or other uses.

community: all the people living in a particular area or place.

5

CITIES

Words to know!

goods: items that can be bought, sold, or traded.

service: work done for others as a job or business, such as a doctor providing medical services.

trading center: a central place where people meet to exchange goods.

commerce: the activity of buying, selling, and trading.

LET'S TRADE!

Soon, people figured out that they could swap **goods** and **services** to get what they needed. A person who made pottery, for example, could trade with someone who made weapons. Some communities became **trading centers**, where people brought their goods to swap with others. As these communities grew, they began to resemble more closely the cities of today—busy areas where **commerce** takes place.

Why some communities became trading centers depended a lot on location. Being near a waterway helped an area get more traffic and grow faster. After all, people didn't want to travel for days across a desert loaded down with goods. They'd much rather float their goods down a river to reach a growing community. As trade expanded to distant parts of the world, access to waterways allowed traders to send their goods on ships and receive shipments from other lands.

A NAME BY ANY OTHER

Once an area was **established**, people needed to call it something to identify it when talking with others. Today, you can often trace the name of a city back to its **origins**.

- Cheektowaga, meaning "land of the crabapples," was named by the Seneca Native Americans in western New York for the small, fruit-bearing trees that grow there.

- Detroit, Michigan, was named after the river linking Lake Huron and Lake Erie. "Detroit" is the French word for "strait," which means a channel of water.

- Oakland, California, got its name because of a thick area of oak trees.

- New York was originally settled by the Dutch and called New Amsterdam after their city in Holland. When the English took control, they changed the name to New York in honor of the Duke of York. The "old" York is a city in England.

- Hershey, Pennsylvania, was named after the chocolate maker Milton Hershey. He opened the world's first modern chocolate **factory** and built the town for its employees and their families to have a place to live, work, and play.

- Today, Mumbai, India, is called by its original name. When Britain controlled the city, it was known as Bombay.

Words to Know!

established: a custom, belief, practice, or place that is recognized after having been in existence for a long enough time.

origin: the place or moment when something comes into existence.

factory: a large place where goods are made.

DID YOU KNOW?

Topeka, Kansas, changed its name to "Google" for one month.

CITIES

A source of fresh water was also important because traveling traders and their thirsty animals needed it to drink. And people who lived in these trading centers needed it to survive. But a trading community also needed to be located near intersections of major travel paths on land, so people not traveling on water could reach them.

As communities grew in size and in wealth, fewer people had to spend long hours growing crops or tending livestock. Some people were free to turn their attention to other things such as education, recreation, arts, religion, and inventions.

Words to know!

society: an organized community of people.

culture: the beliefs and way of life of a group of people.

From skilled craftsmen to laborers and great thinkers, growing towns became the focal point for people who began to transform **societies** and **cultures**. Cities were born— and they would continue to grow and influence the entire world.

KEEPING SAFE

Safety was another important consideration for the growth of a trading center. Communities built on higher ground were more protected against flooding from nearby waterways. People living there could defend themselves more easily against intruders.

There were benefits to living in growing communities. People could easily trade goods without having to travel long distances. There was safety in having a large group of people living in the same place instead of wandering across open land alone.

DID YOU KNOW?

The largest city in the United States is New York, with more than 8 million residents, but the oldest city is St. Augustine, Florida, settled in 1565.

WHAT'S IN A NAME?
CITY NAMING PROJECT

SUPPLIES

☑ paper, cardstock, or index cards

☑ pen or pencil

☑ poster board

☑ colored markers

If you've ever wanted to live in Sarahville or Adamsburg, here's your chance to name your own city!

1 Imagine you are suddenly dropped in the middle of a land without any structures. Brainstorm as many features of that place as you can—these could influence the naming of a new city. Don't stop to think too much, just write everything down. Here are some starting points:

* **Weather**. Is it windy? A blizzard? So hot you can see the air shimmer? Maybe it's always cloudy or rains a lot.

* **Landscape**. What are the features of the land? What kinds of plants are in this land? Pine trees? Cactus? Is it hilly or completely flat? Maybe the river running through it is making a funny sound or perhaps there's a saltwater bay.

* **Inhabitants**. Do the local people speak another language? What do they call the area? What living creatures can you see around you?

* **Businesses**. Maybe there's a cliff filled with precious stones towering nearby. Or maybe the land is the perfect place to start a hang-gliding school. What could you turn into commerce for your new city?

* **Names**. Naming a city after yourself can be fun—but coming up with a twist on your name can be even more interesting! Maybe you can name the city after a friend who's helping you establish the city or an old pet!

2 Go through your brainstorm list and write down at least 10 possible names on index cards. Look them over and decide which you like best. When you've named your city, write it on your poster board and draw a picture of what your new city would look like and why it's called the name you selected.

MAKE YOUR OWN
PHOTO SAFARI

Sometimes we live in a place for so long that we don't even really see it any more. It's hard to imagine what it would look like to someone arriving there for the very first time. With this photo safari, you get the chance to learn a little about the place you call home, whether it's a city or a small town, and see it from the eyes of a **tourist**. **Always have an adult supervise while you are on the Internet.**

1 At the top of your poster board, write the name of your city (or a city nearby or one you've always been interested in). Then, below that, use the ruler to divide the rest of the board into three vertical sections and label them "past," "present," and "future."

Words to know!

tourist: a traveler who visits a place for fun.

2 Visit your local library or do some research online with a parent's supervision. Find out some history of your chosen city. For example:

- ★ When was it settled?
- ★ What was in the area when people first came there? Why did they come?
- ★ How did they choose the name?

3 Put the information you learn under the "past" column. If you can find some old pictures from the area, see if you can copy them to put on your board, too. Or you can get creative and draw pictures!

4 Take pictures of some of the people and places in your city now (or draw them) to put on your board. Write about what's happening today in the city—what it's like, what you like about it, and even what you might not care for. Put as much information as you can in the "present" column.

5 Finally, think a little about what the city might be like in the future. You can make good guesses by checking out the city's Chamber of Commerce site or going to the visitor's center if your city has one. Ask questions of teachers and even people working at the Chamber of Commerce. Maybe you can find out if there are new developments coming, new stores, or any big changes. List everything you find out in the "future" column. You can even draw pictures of what you think things will look like in 10 or 20 years (or more!).

6 Take a look at how things in this city have changed over time and might change in the future. Is it changing in a way that you like? What would you change about it if you could?

FUTURE CITIES: REAL ATLANTIS

There are some pretty crazy ideas about the cities of the future. Like living underwater! For instance, Malaysian architect Sarly Andre Bin Sarkum designed a "seascraper." This building would float in the water like a buoy with just the top above the water's surface. On the roof there would be farms for food and then everybody would live below. The seascraper would even generate its own electricity through wave power! If you could invent your own city, what would it look like? How would things work? Create a travel brochure for this city using brochures you collect or find on the Internet for inspiration.

MAKE YOUR OWN
CITY NAME CHALLENGE

SUPPLIES

☑ Internet access
☑ paper, cardstock, or index cards
☑ pen or pencil

In addition to a city's proper name, many also have nicknames. Some can be pretty funny or descriptive. With this nickname game, you can challenge your friends and family to figure out which nicknames belong to which real cities. **Always have an adult supervise while you are on the Internet.**

1 With supervision from a parent, go online and search for the names of cities and towns around you, along with their nicknames.

2 On the front of each card, write down the real name of the city or town. On the back, write down the nickname.

3 Expand your search to well-known cities and towns, too. These can be from anywhere in the world. Here are some cities to get you started:

* Los Angeles (City of Angels)
* Philadelphia (City of Brotherly Love)
* Seattle (Emerald City)
* New York (The Big Apple)
* Paris (City of Light)
* Amsterdam (Venice of the North)

4 Once you have a stack of at least 20 cards, challenge your friends and family to see who does the best on your city nickname quiz. Show them the city name and have them guess the nickname—or flip it around and see if they can guess the city just from the nickname!

Try This! Here's a fun twist: If you don't find a nickname—and some cities don't have one—challenge yourself, along with your friends and family, to come up with one! You can use the same brainstorming suggestions from the City Naming Project.

CHAPTER 2

Cities Grow Up

When you're approaching a city, does it look real? From a distance, a city can look like it's built from building blocks. The different-sized buildings seem as though they are all lined up against the sky. But when you're standing on a street in the middle of a city, it really hits you. Those buildings are TALL! You could get a sore neck from walking around, looking way up at the tops.

CITIES

Scientists believe the first early cities existed in 4000–3500 BCE in Mesopotamia, such as Eridu and Ur. As more people moved to early cities, they realized they couldn't keep adding more buildings beside each other forever. They would run out of room or run into a river or cliff! So people began to build up.

PILE ON

What happens when cities start to run out of room to spread out? People had to figure out how to build taller buildings. But this isn't easy. The taller the building, the more **stress** is put on the building materials, especially at the lower levels. A building made from stone or brick is extremely heavy. The walls of the lower levels have to be very thick, and a taller building needs even thicker lower walls. Plus, the taller a building, the more **pressure** put on it by the wind.

Words to know!

stress: pressure or strain caused by a large amount of weight.

pressure: a force that pushes on an object.

ANCIENT CITIES

Some ancient cities such as Machu Picchu in Peru (around 1450 CE) and Catal Huyuk in Turkey (around 7500 BCE) didn't even have streets like you recognize in cities and towns today—there was no need for them. There were some footpaths, but the cities were mostly just clusters of structures tightly built alongside each other. Different homes even shared walls! People built their houses from mud bricks and used ladders to get up and down to each level. And in other ancient places, such as Petra in Jordan (around 312 BCE), they built their homes directly into the walls of cliffs.

"STEEL"ING THE SCENE

The Great Pyramid of Giza in Egypt was built more than 4,500 years ago. For thousands of years, it was the tallest structure in the world. It was built of stone, almost 480 feet tall (about 150 meters, or about as tall as one and a half Statues of Liberty), as a grand place for an Egyptian king to be buried in after he died. Stone and brick buildings that people lived and worked in were eventually built as tall as 10 **stories**. That's about as high as half of a football field is long—about 100 feet (about 30.5 meters).

Then, in the mid to late 1800s, inventors figured out new ways to make steel cheaply and easily out of iron. Iron is a strong metal that can be shaped into tools. Steel is mostly iron but it has other **elements** in it to make it much stronger than iron. In stone and brick buildings, each wall of a building is supported by **load-bearing** walls beneath them.

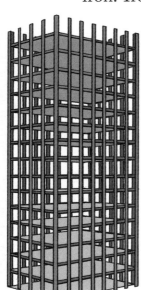

Words to know!

story: a floor in a building.

element: a substance that cannot be broken down into a simpler substance, such as oxygen and gold. Everything is made up of combinations of elements.

load-bearing: supporting the bulk of the weight of a structure.

By using steel, a metal frame could support the weight of the walls and windows. Steel-framed buildings were lighter and far stronger than any building frames ever built. Around the same time, an elevator brake was invented by Elisha Otis. The elevator brake made elevators much safer because it stopped an elevator from falling if its cable broke. Now people had a way to build taller buildings—and a way to safely get up to and down from the upper floors!

RACE YOU TO THE TOP!

Once **engineers** had the ability to make taller and taller buildings, it became a competition to see who could build the tallest skyscraper. Early on, companies such as Sears, Chrysler, and Metropolitan Life built skyscrapers so their names would be associated with the superstructures.

Because everyone was so competitive and wanted the tallest building, there had to be rules about what counts toward a building's height. Should only the floors of the building count? What about **antennae** and **spires**? These can add hundreds of feet to the height of a building.

Buildings are ranked in many ways: by the height of the structure, the height of the highest floor, and the height to the top of any part, like a spire. But when height is officially calculated to name the tallest building, antennae do not count, because they can be added or removed without changing the structure of the building. Spires do count because they are permanent.

For many years, New York City held the record for the tallest building, first with the Empire State Building and then with the World Trade Center. But in 1974, the Sears Tower was built in Chicago. For 24 years it was the tallest building in the world, at 1,454 feet (443 meters). When the Petronas Towers were built in Malaysia, the 1,476-foot-tall buildings (450 meters) took the "tallest skyscraper" rank out of the United States for the first time.

Words to know!

engineer: someone who designs or builds things such as roads, bridges, and buildings.

antenna: a metal rod on a building used to receive radio or television signals.

spire: a pointy structure that decorates the top of a building.

DID YOU KNOW?

The Petronas Towers in Malaysia are the tallest twin towers in the world. They have a skybridge connecting them.

Chicago, London, and New York City all competed to build taller and taller buildings, called skyscrapers. These cities were all short on space and big on growth. But there was also a little friendly competition there. Each city wanted the most impressive buildings. Skyscrapers were awe-inspiring and people loved to see the soaring buildings. It made them proud of their city.

DID YOU KNOW?

The Willis Tower in Chicago (formerly the Sears Tower) is so tall you can see four states from the top: Illinois, Indiana, Wisconsin, and Michigan. And there are six robotic window-washing machines that clean the windows to help you see clearly!

WHAT'S THAT SMELL?

While cities grew upwards during the late 1800s and early 1900s, they were experiencing growing pains. Millions of people flooded in to find jobs and start new lives, **immigrating** from other countries and moving from rural areas. This made cities more and more crowded and dirty and smelly. Most of the people in a city lived packed into small buildings. A family might live with two or three other families in one apartment in a building called a **tenement**.

Words to know!

immigrate: to move from one country to live in another.

tenement: a multi-family living space, usually occupied by poor people.

Because there were so many people living so close together, problems often popped up in the crowded conditions. How did people cook? Where did they bathe and go to the bathroom? What did they do with their trash? Where did they sleep?

Words to know!

plumbing: the pipes that carry water in and out of a building.

outhouse: an outdoor toilet built over a hole in the ground.

fire escape: a metal stairway on the outside of a building used to escape a fire.

trolley: a large cart.

For heat and cooking, everyone shared a wood-burning stove. For those lucky enough to have indoor **plumbing**, the one bathroom was shared by all the families in the apartment or by several apartments. Otherwise, the bathroom was an **outhouse** in the back of the building. Sometimes people just threw their garbage right out the window into the street! If it was really hot at night, you might crawl out through the window and sleep on the **fire escape** with your sisters and brothers.

You might not go to school because your family needed you to work. Many children and their parents worked in factories. Factory jobs were dangerous and didn't pay a lot of money.

Until early in the 1900s, people moved around the city by horse-drawn **trolleys**. That meant a lot of horse manure piling up in the streets—yuck! When the automobile was invented, more and more people drove around the city. But you had to watch out if you were in the street. Without set traffic rules, it was everyone for himself or herself out there!

CITY PLANNING

Ancient city planners as far back as 5000 BCE in areas such as today's Egypt, Pakistan, and Iraq wanted their cities to be orderly and functional. Most chose to lay out their city in a grid pattern. With this system, buildings and roads are laid out into block formations. Roads are straight, and most run east to west or north to south. Planned cities have been laid out in this way for thousands of years. To make it easier for people to find their way, cities often name the streets in a grid system **numerically** or **alphabetically**. Many of Manhattan's streets in New York City are named this way.

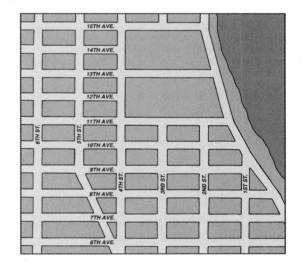

Words to know!

numerically: in order by number—1, 2, 3, etc.

alphabetically: in order by letter—a, b, c, etc.

adapt: changes a person, plant, or animal makes to survive.

But why don't all cities follow this pattern? Because not all cities are planned. Boston's roads were **adapted** from existing horse and cart paths from the seventeenth century. Other roads were added as the city grew. But if you go to Back Bay in Boston, you'll find a small section of the city that does follow this grid pattern. The east-west streets in Back Bay are in alphabetical order: Arlington, Berkeley, Clarendon, Dartmouth, Exeter, Fairfield, Gloucester, and Hereford.

Washington, DC, is laid out in a grid system, but there are also roads that run diagonally, cutting across the city like wheel spokes. Traffic circles direct the movement around these areas.

MAKE YOUR OWN
CITY PLANNING GAME

Although ancient city planners made things look easy, sometimes designing a city isn't as easy as just drawing a grid and you're done. You need to think about obstacles or how things might change over time. With this game, test yourself to see if you've got what it takes to plan a city.

1 Mark the poster board into a grid with squares about 2 inches long on each side (5 centimeters). To do this, mark across the top every 2 inches, then down the side every 2 inches. Use the ruler as a guide to draw connecting lines. This will be the base of your city.

2 On your scrap paper or index cards, measure and cut squares and rectangles that will fit onto the graph you just made. For example, make a rectangle that measures 2 inches (5 centimeters) by 6 inches (15 centimeters), or a square that measures 4 inches by 4 inches (10 centimeters). Cut out several different sizes.

3 On your squares and rectangles, draw or write features that a city planner would normally include. For example:

* River
* Roads
* Lake
* Train tracks
* Hospital
* Apartments

4 You will want to make several cards for some features, such as roads and apartment buildings. When you have 30 or more features, you're ready to start. You can play alone or with a partner, but you're not competing with each other. You're working together to build the city.

5 Randomly draw cards from your feature pile. Decide where you're going to position them on your city grid (poster board) and put them there.

6 When you've placed all your cards, notice the layout you chose. Did you use a grid pattern, or let the roads form naturally? Name your roads.

7 Did you make any changes to your planning as you went along? You might not put residential buildings right next to the railroad track, for instance. The people would complain about all the noise! Putting them next to the city park would probably be a great move for your residents, though.

Try This! Now try thinking about the smaller details of the city. What are the differences between the places that people live and the places that people work? Where should things such as restaurants and movie theaters go? What about very small things such as benches, fountains, and trees? Play again with even more cards. Try to make your city a place where everyone would want to live.

MAKE YOUR OWN
SKYSCRAPER CHALLENGE

SUPPLIES

- ☑ thin cardboard, such as from cereal boxes
- ☑ scissors
- ☑ ruler
- ☑ tape
- ☑ popsicle sticks
- ☑ wood glue or super glue
- ☑ a heavy object, such as a thick book or can of soup

The first buildings in cities weren't very tall. The materials that were used weren't strong enough. Now that engineers use steel, they can build skyscrapers. With this project, you will see which materials work for homemade skyscrapers and which materials definitely don't!

1 Cut the thin cardboard into large square pieces all the same size. Use the ruler to make sure all sides are the same length. These will be the walls and ceilings of your first skyscraper.

2 Using the tape, connect five pieces of cardboard to construct the first floor of a building (four walls and a top). Then use another four walls and top to build another story on top of the first. Connect the stories with tape. Continue adding stories until your skyscraper is as tall as you want. Set this building aside for now.

3 With the popsicle sticks, build a frame for a second building. To build one wall, lay four sticks into a square and attach them with glue. Then take another pair of sticks and glue them in a "+" shape on top of the square. You now have one wall. Continue to make three more walls, then tape them together into the first floor of your building.

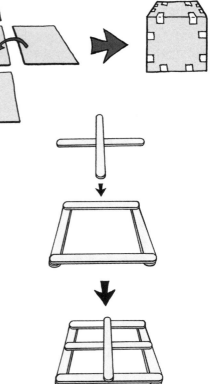

4 Attach pieces of cardboard to your new building's framework. The roof story will be just cardboard. Assemble another story the same way you did the first, with squares and +s. Attach this story on top of the first with tape.

5 Continue building until your second building is as tall as the first.

6 Making sure the glue has dried completely, place your heavy object on top of the first building made from just cardboard. What happens? Does it hold the weight and stay standing? If so, how much more weight can you put on top?

7 Try putting the same object on top of the second building—your "steel-framed" skyscraper. How much weight can it hold? Is it more than the first building? Is a framed building stronger than a building without a frame?

Try This! Think about features and materials that can make your skyscraper even stronger. Will more popsicle sticks make the structure stronger or weigh it down? How does the thickness of the cardboard affect the amount of weight your skyscraper can hold? What could you do to the base of your building to make it even stronger? Try different things until your skyscraper is tall and strong.

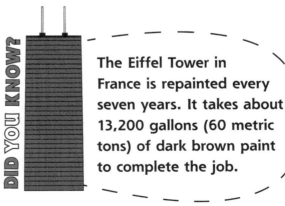

DID YOU KNOW?

The Eiffel Tower in France is repainted every seven years. It takes about 13,200 gallons (60 metric tons) of dark brown paint to complete the job.

- 23 -

MAKE YOUR OWN
3D CITY MODEL

Use the city planning poster board from the earlier project to really bring your city to life. You can see it "grow" right before your eyes.

1 If you planned a city with the City Planning Game project, lay it out on a flat surface. If you didn't make one, draw a proposed city—with whatever street system you choose—onto poster board.

2 Use the building supplies to transform your diagram into a 3D city. You might run into unexpected problems. For instance, maybe one of your features was a river, but now you find it's completely encircling an apartment building. *Yikes!* How will people get in and out? Solve problems like these with small pieces such as bridges and walkways.

3 Tape or glue your city to the poster board if you'd like.

Try This! Once you've designed your 3D city, think about the heights of your buildings and where they're located. For instance, do you want really tall skyscrapers surrounding a park? Should the tall buildings be bunched together or spread out across the city? Where is the best place to put the shortest buildings? Keep experimenting until you think you've made the best choices.

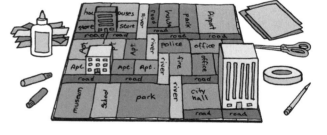

Bringing Power to the People

Have you spent time in a city at night? While rural areas are quiet and dark at night, cities are busy and brightly lit. People enjoy shopping, eating out in restaurants, and other fun activities such as going to the theater. New York City has so much going on at night that it is nicknamed "The City That Never Sleeps."

The bright lights of a city—from streetlamps, apartment buildings, stores, theaters, and office buildings—make a beautiful sight at night.

BUT WHAT DOES IT TAKE TO POWER A CITY? WHERE DOES ALL THAT ELECTRICITY COME FROM?

LET THERE BE LIGHT

Before the 1800s, candles and oil lamps were the only sources of light for people. Because candles don't give off a lot of light, cities were as dark as a forest at night. By the mid-1800s, cities had

lights fueled by gas that made it a lot easier to see at night than before. These gaslights were in lamps placed on poles or attached to buildings.

DID YOU KNOW?

London and Boston and many other cities still use some gas-lit streetlights to preserve the history of certain areas such as Boston's Beacon Hill and Bay Village and outside Buckingham Palace in London.

But the gaslights were spaced far apart and weren't very bright. For most people in cities, nighttime was a time to stay at home. Most streets were dark and the city was a dangerous place to walk around at night.

In the late nineteenth century, the use of electricity became possible with Thomas Edison's invention of the light bulb. In 1882, Edison "flipped the switch" on an electric power station in New York City, giving the United States its first electrically lit buildings in lower Manhattan. Electric lights began popping up everywhere. Finally, people could feel safe walking outside at night.

But there was a problem. Edison's electric system used **direct current (DC)**. Because electricity could only travel in one direction along the wires in a DC system, it had to move directly from the **generator** to the lights.

Words to know!

direct current (DC): electricity that flows in one direction.

generator: a machine that converts mechanical energy into electricity.

alternating current (AC): electricity that flows back and forth at a steady rate.

For everyone in a city to use DC electricity, it had to be generated very close to the buildings using it. Electricity generated too far away from a building would arrive too weak to power all of its lights. Edison proposed placing many large generators around to distribute the electricity. But this would cost a lot of money and mean that many power stations would have to be built throughout each city. Another idea was to install massive copper wires—which conduct electricity without losing much energy—all around the city. This solution would also cost a lot of money—and would be ugly, too!

THE BEST SOLUTION WAS PROPOSED BY NIKOLA TESLA. HE WORKED WITH ALTERNATING CURRENT (AC), WHICH ALTERNATES ELECTRICITY IN BOTH DIRECTIONS ALONG A SINGLE WIRE.

AC is more **efficient** than DC. It allows higher **voltages** to travel farther and doesn't require as many energy stations. A **transformer** placed between the customer and the generator changes the voltage to a lower level that the customer can use.

Words to know!

efficient: making the most of time and energy.

voltage: the force that moves electricity along a wire.

transformer: a device that changes the voltage of electricity.

reduce: to use less of something.

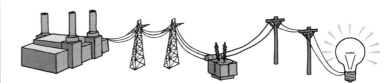

Today's cities use a network of electricity called a power grid. Power is generated at an electrical plant. This high-voltage power is sent to thousands of transformers, which **reduce** the voltage. The power is then sent through thousands of miles of cables, usually underground, to the people who use it.

In the future, power may again be generated close to or on the buildings using it, with renewable energy from the sun, wind, and other sources.

LIGHTS OUT

Widespread power outages are rare in big cities because different substations provide electricity to different areas. Most of the time, only some stations lose power, affecting only some areas of a city. A power outage can cause big problems! When traffic lights are out, how are drivers supposed to know when it's their turn to go? Schools need lights and heat or air conditioning to run smoothly. Hospitals have to use generators to make emergency electricity to keep patients safe—or alive. Unless residents, restaurants, and grocery stores have other means of storing and cooking food, no electricity means food can spoil quickly.

WHAT'S DOWN THERE?

In big cities, most of the electrical cables and transformers are underground. Workers access them through the round **manholes** in the streets. The workers go down ladders into the space underground, which is usually around 8 feet (about 2½ meters) deep. There, they can work with the cables that run under the street.

Words to know!

manhole: a round opening that provides access below a street.

SOMETIMES THE JOB CAN GET MESSY. THOSE MANHOLE COVERS DON'T KEEP OUT DIRT AND WATER!

DID YOU KNOW?

Metal manhole covers weigh anywhere from 80 to 100 pounds (36 to 45 kilograms)! They're round instead of square so they don't accidentally fall into the hole.

Water can seep in, and if the service area gets too muddy or filled with water, workers call a "flush truck" to run clean water through the space, then suck it all out.

OH, SAY, CAN YOU SEE?

Streetlights have been used for more than 2,000 years, whether to light paths so travelers don't stumble or just to illuminate the dark night against robbers. In the United States, inventor Benjamin Franklin was the first to light the streets with lamps. He created a street lamp that was a four-sided glass lantern protecting a candle. It was someone's job to light all the street lamps in the evening and then **extinguish** them at dawn.

In the late 1700s, gas lighting appeared on streets around the world. Baltimore was the first city in the United States to start using gas streetlights. With the invention of the electric light bulb, streetlights were lit using electricity instead of gas for power.

Words to know!

extinguish: to put out.
migrate: to move from one place to another when seasons change.

Although streetlights provide safety, they can cause problems for people driving at night. When people drive in the dark, the pupils in their eyes expand to let in as much light as possible so they can see further. If they suddenly drive into a brightly lit area, their pupils constrict, or get smaller, very quickly. This means they can't see well while their eyes adjust, which can be a dangerous thing.

In early 2013, a law was passed in France that requires cities—including Paris—to turn off window lighting in stores and businesses after 1:00 am. Interior lighting, such as in office buildings, needs to be shut off when the last employee leaves. This is not only to save money (about the equivalent electricity use of 750,000 households!) but also to help protect against light pollution.

Another problem with very brightly lit areas is the way they can confuse **migrating** birds and sea turtles. In some areas where this is an issue, streetlights are dimmed so they don't distract wildlife.

DID YOU KNOW?

The world's first public electrical grid was built in 1881 in the town of Godalming, England.

MAKE YOUR OWN
DC CURRENT BATTERY

With DC electricity, the flow of energy is in one direction, like a river. The batteries you put in your flashlight are DC current. You can create your own DC current battery out of a lemon! **Caution: This activity requires the use of a knife, so ask an adult to supervise.**

SUPPLIES

☑ lemon

☑ knife

☑ penny

☑ dime

☑ 2 pieces of thin copper wire, each about 1 foot (30½ centimeters) long

☑ miniature LED bulb

1 Loosen the juice inside the lemon by firmly rolling it around between your palm and a table.

2 Cut two small slits in the lemon just long enough to hold the coins by their edges. Stick the penny into one slot and the dime into the other. The coins should fit snugly.

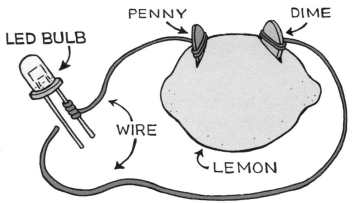

3 Wrap one end of one piece of wire around the penny. Attach the other end to the light bulb.

4 Attach the other wire to both the dime and the light bulb. Does your "electric lemon" make the light glow?

What's Happening? Electricity is flowing through the wires. The acid in the lemon reacts with the different metals in the coins. That creates a one-way electrical flow—a DC current. Positive particles are pulled to one metal and negative particles are pulled to the other. What happens when you use a lime? What about an orange or a grape? See how the different fruits affect the light bulb. What do the reactions tell you about each fruit?

MAKE YOUR OWN
POWER GRID GAME

SUPPLIES

☑ deck of playing cards
☑ dominoes
☑ three small toy buildings

Because of the way power is distributed throughout a city, when one area loses power it affects a larger area. That's why you have "power outages." Something may have happened miles from where you live, but your power is still affected. For instance, a tree limb may fall on a power line two blocks away and break the flow of electricity to your neighborhood. With this game, you will create a main energy path and a backup plan—but be careful! If one power line goes down, the people in your city might lose power. In this game, design your power grid to keep as many buildings powered up as possible!

1 Remove the following cards from your deck: anything numbered six or higher and all the face cards except two jacks and one king. You will play the game with the remaining cards.

2 Place your three buildings according to the diagram. You have one energy station and two buildings that receive power.

3 To play, take turns drawing cards. If you get a number card, place as many dominoes on the "power grid" as indicated, following the diagram here. You can also make up your own diagram. Just be sure the paths go from the energy station to the buildings.

4 If you draw the king, you can start a new backup branch from the main energy station.

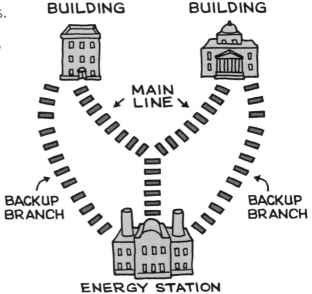

5 If you draw a jack, look out—there has been a disruption to your power grid. Push over one of the domino paths, either the backup or the main line. You'll need to start rebuilding that path again.

6 If you get to the bottom of your card deck without finishing, just shuffle the deck and start over.

7 Your objective is to build your power grid to your businesses without any disruption. At least two of your paths—the main line and a backup—should stay intact.

Try This! Add a few more buildings to the diagram to make the game more difficult. Decide what kinds of buildings they are—homes, schools, stores, skyscrapers, city government buildings, the fire department. Which buildings should be connected to the backup power branches? Are some buildings, such as hospitals, more important than others? Why?

Words to know!

sub-Saharan Africa: the part of Africa that is south of the Sahara Desert.

DID YOU KNOW?

Cities use a lot of energy. Midtown Manhattan uses more than the entire country of Kenya, and New York State uses more than all of **sub-Saharan Africa** put together.

CHAPTER 4
Water Challenges

Where does the water from your faucet actually come from? In rural areas, people often get their water from private wells. In small towns, people might get their water from a giant water tank. But what about in cities? With millions of people needing water every day, a tank would dry up very quickly. And there's no room for all those private wells. So how do people in cities get water?

WHEN IN ROME . . .

In ancient times, bringing water to cities was very difficult. Water had to be carried miles to reach the residents, which was hard, slow work. As a solution, around 700 BCE the talented engineers of ancient Rome created the **aqueduct**.

An aqueduct is a **canal** of water that transports water from its source to the people who need it, usually for drinking or for watering crops. Because water flows downhill, an aqueduct is always positioned slightly lower than its source. Aqueducts often look like bridges full of water.

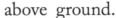

Words to know!

aqueduct: a channel that transports water from its source over a great distance.

canal: a man-made channel used to deliver water.

The wealthiest people of Rome were lucky enough to have the water from aqueducts run directly into their homes. Everyone else had to get their water from public fountains in the city.

Many ancient aqueducts are still standing in Europe, the Middle East, and South America. Modern water systems are underground and made from pipes, instead of carved from stone and located above ground.

Today, few cities get their water through aqueducts. Instead, water is brought into cities through a series of pipes and tanks. The city of Los Angeles, California, is supplied by three of these major underground water pipelines.

WHERE SHOULD I PUT THIS?

Though cities could now bring fresh water in through aqueducts, another problem remained. Where should the dirty, used water go?

Ancient cities didn't have toilets that flushed. Getting rid of **wastewater** wasn't as easy as just flushing it away the way we do in our bathrooms today. That's why ancient cities built public **latrines**. These were often just long trenches dug in the ground.

SOMETIMES THE TRENCHES WERE COVERED WITH LONG STONE BENCHES WITH HOLES CUT IN THEM FOR PEOPLE TO SIT ON.

Unlike in public restrooms today, there was no privacy in these public latrines. And although the waste was washed away by flowing water beneath them, the

Words to know!

wastewater: water that has been used by people in their homes, in factories, and in other businesses and is now dirty.

latrine: a bathroom that can be used by several people at once, often as simple as a long trench dug in the earth.

unsanitary: something that is dirty and unhealthy.

chamber pot: a large, bowl-shaped pot used as an indoor toilet.

latrines were still **unsanitary** and could easily spread disease. At home, people in cities used **chamber pots** instead of the public latrines. These large pots with a hole in the top were used as individual toilets. When it was time to empty it, many people just dumped all of the waste out the window.

THIS METHOD OF EMPTYING WASTE BECAME SUCH A PROBLEM THAT LAWS WERE PASSED TO STOP IT FROM HAPPENING.

By law, people had to dump their chamber pots into large community vats. This was more work, but it made the streets a lot cleaner!

BIRTH OF THE SEWER

Wastewater doesn't just smell bad, it's also quite dangerous. If it isn't thrown away properly, wastewater can contribute to the spread of diseases, especially in crowded places like cities.

Words to know!

sewer: a drain for wastewater.

treatment plant: where wastewater is sent through a cleaning process.

In ancient Rome, the main **sewer** was called the Cloaca Maxima, which means "Greatest Sewer." It ran above the ground and was fed by streams from nearby hills. The sewer washed waste away from the city and into the nearby Tiber River.

ANCIENT ROME
▬ = CLOACA MAXIMA
TIBER RIVER

Today, sewers are a system of pipes that run underground, carrying wastewater away from homes and businesses. The dirty water doesn't flow into natural bodies of water anymore. First, the water is sent to a **treatment plant**.

TREAT ME WELL!

Wastewater goes through a series of processes at the treatment plant. To clean it, all of the water's **contaminants** must be removed. The contaminants are removed in different ways, through both physical and chemical processes. **It takes three steps to clean wastewater.**

First, the water is held in a still area. This lets solid materials settle to the bottom. Lighter contaminants, such as oil, float to the top. Once these materials are removed, the rest of the water is treated with the next process.

The next treatment gets rid of any **biological** matter in the water. This is done by natural **microorganisms**, such as bacteria, that feed on the waste. The microorganisms are filtered out after they've done their job.

The final treatment gets rid of any contaminants that are left. This is done chemically or physically, in a process called **microfiltration**.

Words to know!

contaminant: any pollutant or object that could harm a living organism.

biological: anything that is or was living.

microorganism: a living thing that is so tiny it can only be seen using a microscope. Bacteria, fungi, and algae are all microorganisms.

microfiltration: to filter something using extremely fine filters.

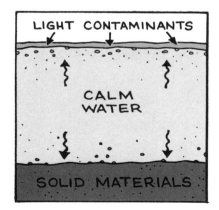

LIGHT CONTAMINANTS

CALM WATER

SOLID MATERIALS

MICROORGANISMS FEEDING ON WASTE

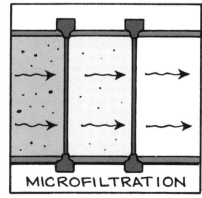

MICROFILTRATION

After water has been processed at a treatment plant, it is clean enough to be used for **irrigation** or to be sent to a natural body of water such as a river or a lake.

THIRSTY UP HERE

If water always flows down, how do people get their water at the very top of a skyscraper?

Engineers solve this problem with a series of **pumps**. Water piled up on itself is under pressure. This means that water at the bottom of a skyscraper is under stronger pressure and will come out of the faucet more forcefully than the water at the top, where there's not as much water weight pushing down.

The water pumps throughout skyscrapers give water at all levels of the building the same amount of pressure.

Words to know!

irrigation: a system of transporting water through canals or tunnels to water crops.

pump: a device that moves water or other liquids.

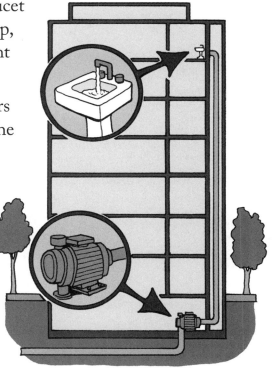

DID YOU KNOW?

Americans use 2.5 million plastic water bottles an hour. Each bottle takes 500 years to decompose! Drinking tap water instead of bottled water helps the environment.

THIRSTY DESERT CITY

It's not hard to imagine that a city surrounded by lakes and **reservoirs** has a water supply. But what if a city is surrounded by dry desert? How does it get water?

Phoenix, Arizona, is an example of a city in a desert. With little rainfall and few natural water sources, the residents need to think very carefully about how they get and use water.

Phoenix has a network of canals that moves water from the nearby Salt River Dam to water treatment facilities. From there, a smaller canal network is controlled by city workers. They'll open these up to let water flow to use in landscaping.

Words to know!

reservoir: a manmade or natural lake used to collect water that can be stored for future use.

xeriscaping: landscaping with rocks and plants that need very little or no water.

To make sure there's enough water for the more than 3.5 million people who live in Phoenix, all of the residents have to do their part. For example, residents are asked to do their laundry at night so there's more water available during the day. Residents are also asked to practice **xeriscaping**. Since grass needs a lot of water, people instead use attractive rocks or native desert plants for their lawns. They also use special barrels that capture rain and low-pressure water heads in their showers. Agricultural fields are angled to collect the water runoff.

DID YOU KNOW?

Your toilet is musical! Most toilets flush in E flat.

Today, despite its growth, Phoenix uses less water than it did 10 years ago. And if this desert city can do it, cities with enough water supplies can too!

MAKE YOUR OWN
ANCIENT AQUEDUCT

Cities used aqueducts to get water from nearby sources. Some aqueducts crossed many miles. The aqueducts had to be at just the right slope to get the water to flow well without coming out the other end too fast. You can experiment with your own aqueduct with this project.

SUPPLIES

- ☑ modeling clay
- ☑ spoon
- ☑ yardstick
- ☑ bowl or container
- ☑ pitcher
- ☑ water

1 Use the modeling clay to make four short thick legs for the aqueduct. You can make more if you want a longer aqueduct. Make sure the legs are solid and not too tall.

2 Set your aqueduct legs aside and use the clay to make a long, thick rope. Make it just a bit longer than your finished aqueduct will be.

3 Laying your clay rope flat on the table, use the spoon to dig a deep trench into the length of your rope. It's okay if you flatten the bottom of your rope, just make sure there are no holes and the sides of your aqueduct are high enough so water won't spill over the edges.

4 Set your aqueduct legs in an evenly spaced row. Lay the yardstick across the top of them for support. Then lay your aqueduct on top of the yardstick.

5 Position your receiving bowl at the end of the aqueduct so the water will fall into it. Then carefully begin pouring water into the beginning of your aqueduct. Pour slowly and watch closely. Is the water flowing to the container? If not, adjust the angle of your aqueduct. If the water is spilling out, adjust the sides. And if it's coming out the end too fast, lower the angle. Otherwise, the citizens of your city will be flooded!

EXPERIMENT WITH WATER FILTRATION

Scientists and engineers are always working to find the best way to filter wastewater to keep people and the environment safe and clean. With this project, you'll test different types of filter materials to discover which ones would be most effective for your city.

SUPPLIES

- ☑ 2-liter plastic bottle
- ☑ scissors
- ☑ filter materials such as sand, gravel, coffee filter, sponge, cotton, activated charcoal from aquarium store
- ☑ paper and pencil
- ☑ contamination materials such as twigs, ripped paper, soil, dried beans
- ☑ water
- ☑ measuring cup
- ☑ pitcher
- ☑ stopwatch

1 Cut the plastic bottle in half and remove the cap. Turn the top half upside down and put it inside the bottom half.

2 Place one type of filter material inside the top section. Don't use all of your materials at once because you want to test one material at a time.

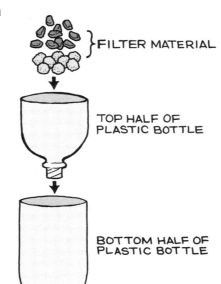

FILTER MATERIAL

TOP HALF OF PLASTIC BOTTLE

BOTTOM HALF OF PLASTIC BOTTLE

3 Once your filter material is in place, add the contaminants. You can put several in at a time or just one type. Real wastewater usually has a lot of different contaminants that need to be filtered out at the same time.

4 Make a chart to record your results. There should be one column to note the filtration material, one for the amount of waste filtered, and one for the time it took to filter the water.

5 Pour four cups of water over the contaminants and filter. Start your stopwatch and watch the bottom to see what gets filtered out.

Filtration Material	Amount of Waste	Time to Filter
Sand		
Gravel		
Coffee Filter		
Sponge		
Cotton		
Charcoal		

6 Stop your watch when the water stops flowing and turns to dripping. Write down what you observe on your chart. How much of the waste was filtered out? How long did it take to filter the water?

7 Empty your materials out and repeat using different filter materials. Use the same contaminants for each test. Record your results.

8 When you're finished, look at what you've found. Was some material easier to filter out? Were some filters more effective than others?

Try This! Can you think of other materials that might make a good filter? Test them out. See what happens when you combine two or three filter materials. Are more contaminants filtered out? Does the process take more or less time? Keep combining filters until you've found the best combination.

MAKE YOUR OWN
WATER PRESSURE EXPERIMENT

With this experiment, you will see how the pressure of water changes depending on how much water is on top of it. Why do the floors at the top of a 30-story skyscraper need different pumps than floors at the bottom? **Caution: This activity requires the use of a knife, so ask an adult to supervise.**

1 Take the top off the empty jug and set it aside. Use the marker to make your jug into a skyscraper. You can draw windows and doors, and even draw the people inside.

2 Have an adult help cut three holes, about as wide as a dime, into the jug. One hole should be close to the bottom of the jug. The next one should be in the middle, and the last one at the top.

3 After you've made the holes, use the modeling clay to make plugs to close them. Tie the string to the top of the jug. It should be long enough that you can hold the jug by the string so it doesn't touch the ground.

4 Take your skyscraper jug and a pitcher of water outside. This will get a bit messy!

5 Carefully fill the jug with water. Tie the jug to a tree branch or fence post.

6 Now quickly remove all the plugs at the same time and watch the water flow. How does the stream of water coming from the bottom hole look compared to the top hole? What about the one in the middle?

What's Happening? The difference in water pressure affects the way the water squirts out of the holes. The stronger the squirt, the more water pressure. You can see why people at the top of a skyscraper need pumps to get water and why people at the bottom don't.

Try This! What happens if you poke more holes in the jug? Does this increase the water pressure or decrease it? Experiment with a smaller jug. Does the water squirt out as far as it did from the big jug?

HOW'S THE WATER UP THERE?

In the early 1900s, water was distributed in tall buildings by a tank on the roof—gravity delivered the water to the floors below. When the tank's water level dropped, a pump brought more water up. One problem with this was the tanks had to be heated in the winter to keep from freezing. And in the summer, the water would be hot from sitting in the sun.

In the 1950s, pressure tank systems powered by an air compressor replaced the roof tanks. This system was indoors and the compressor pumped water to each floor. But the systems used a lot of energy, took up a lot of space, and were expensive to install.

Today, most buildings use a series of pipes and tanks in the walls and basement. Pressure valves on different floors control the water flow, turning on when water is needed on any floor, and shutting off during periods of less use, such as during the night when everyone is sleeping.

CHAPTER 5

Getting Around
Above Ground

City streets are bustling with people and vehicles moving this way and that way. Trucks need to make their deliveries to businesses and restaurants. Buses and taxis bring people where they need to go. People walk to work or the store and others go by bicycle. Police cars, ambulances, and fire trucks are all over the city transporting emergency workers to crime scenes, accidents, and fires.

How is all of the busy movement in cities organized? Because buses, trucks, taxis, cars, bicycles, and pedestrians are crowding the city streets day and night, there have to be set patterns to the traffic. Otherwise, there would be accidents all over the place!

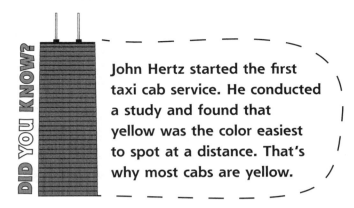

DID YOU KNOW?

John Hertz started the first taxi cab service. He conducted a study and found that yellow was the color easiest to spot at a distance. That's why most cabs are yellow.

THE FIRST ROADS WERE WELL-WORN DIRT PATHS. SUPPLIES AND TRADE GOODS WERE CARRIED OR DRAGGED.

MUD BRICK

CRUSHED STONE

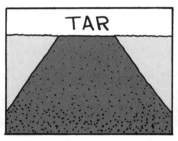
TAR

WOOD PLANKS

With the invention of the wheel around 4000 BCE, goods could be transported by cart, but the roads they used quickly got muddy and rutted and very uncomfortable to travel on.

Over time, people figured out how to use different materials to construct roads that lasted longer. At first the roads in ancient cities in Egypt were built from mud bricks. In Rome, they used thick layers of crushed stone to pave roads. People in the Middle East used tar for their roads. In early America, roads were often made from planks of wood. Though different, these roads were made for the same purpose: To get people in, out, and around growing cities.

PAVE THE WAY

Today, most roads are made of **asphalt**. This dark, sticky tar is usually mixed with other materials such as **concrete**, sand, or crushed stone. The mixture is heated up and poured onto the road's surface, then smoothed and compacted to make a road surface that is durable when it cools and hardens.

City streets are usually made with many layers. The top layers are made of asphalt, each about 2 inches (5 centimeters) thick. Underneath the asphalt is often a layer of concrete. Clay, gravel, or dirt can also be used instead of concrete. Concrete can be used as a road surface too. But concrete isn't as rugged and flexible as asphalt, so it cracks and breaks more easily over time.

Words to know!

asphalt: a black tar that is used to pave roads.

concrete: a hard construction material made with cement, sand, and water.

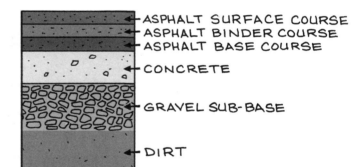

ASPHALT SURFACE COURSE
ASPHALT BINDER COURSE
ASPHALT BASE COURSE
CONCRETE
GRAVEL SUB-BASE
DIRT

GETTING AROUND TOWN

With all of the traffic on city streets, how do people know where and when to cross the street without getting in an accident? Traffic lights are constantly directing drivers and pedestrians so that everyone can travel safely. These lights don't turn red and green randomly. They're carefully timed so that traffic will flow smoothly without any jams. A traffic jam on one city block can quickly create traffic jams on blocks all around it.

TRAFFIC SIGNALS WERE INVENTED IN THE EARLY 1900S IN AMERICA.

At first, there were only two colors: red for stop and green for go. There was also a buzzer to warn drivers that the light was changing. Later, the buzzer was replaced by a yellow light that flashes before the red light.

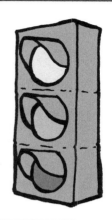

HOLE IN THE ROAD

Have you ever been riding in your parents' car, sipping your bottle of water, when suddenly . . . ca-chunk! You've hit a pothole, and now your mouthful of water is all over your shirt. Asphalt doesn't last forever. Over time, big dents or holes called potholes form in the road. A pothole is created when water standing on the road freezes. When water freezes into ice, it expands. The expanded ice creates cracks in the surface of the asphalt.

When the ice melts, it seeps into these new cracks in the asphalt. The ice water softens the asphalt even more. The water also seeps into the material beneath the asphalt— usually gravel or soil—and softens that, too. As more vehicles drive over this area, the surface asphalt begins to break apart and come loose. The loose pieces of asphalt are knocked away by more vehicles, uncovering the material beneath the asphalt—and there's a pothole!

Large or deep potholes can be dangerous for drivers. Vehicles can be damaged if they are driven over potholes at high speeds. If drivers swerve to miss a pothole, they could hit another car or drive off the road. That's why cities are always paving and re-paving their roads.

Words to know!

automated: controlled by a computer instead of by a person.

synchronized: working together in a pattern.

Early traffic lights were controlled by people who would physically turn a streetlight box so traffic would see either red or green in their direction as they approached. As more and more traffic lights were used, they became **automated**, meaning machines controlled them rather than people. They then became more **synchronized** to keep traffic flowing smoothly down the length of a road and its intersecting streets. Timers or sensors in the roads would automatically give streets with more traffic longer amounts of time to travel through the intersection, to keep traffic from jamming up with too many vehicles waiting for the light to change.

THE PATTERN OF TRAFFIC LIGHTS CHANGES DEPENDING ON THE TIME OF DAY.

COLOR-CODED COMMUNICATION

In the United States, even if you're in an unfamiliar area or have difficulty reading, you still have a good chance of understanding street signs. That's because certain types of signs are always a specific color. For example:

- Green signs with white letters are street names or information signs, for example, distances to the next town or place names.

- Red signs mean stop or are a warning not to do something, like "Do Not Enter."

- Brown signs identify historic or scenic points.

- Yellow signs are warning signs, like "School Zone Ahead."

Each day has two "rush hours," which is when **commuters** travel. The first is in the morning when lots of people travel to work or school, and the second is when they are traveling home. All of these people traveling around 8:00 or 9:00 in the morning and around 5:00 or 6:00 in the evening means much more traffic than usual. So traffic lights on main roads usually stay green longer. This lets a lot more traffic pass through these main roads quickly, clearing out any backups and helping to prevent traffic jams.

Words to know!

commuters: the people who go to work every morning and then home every evening during the week.

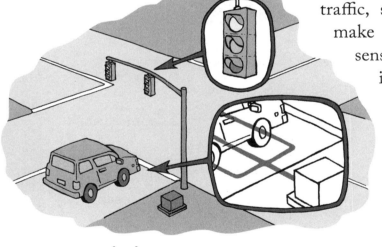

During times when there is less traffic, sensors under the road can make the lights change. These sensors can detect the metal in cars passing above them. When a car drives up to a red light, the sensor underneath the pavement will send a message that the car is waiting, making the light turn green.

DID YOU KNOW?

Do you think that if you have a red light, the other traffic has a green light? There are actually a few seconds when BOTH lights are red. This helps prevent accidents—in case someone decides to "run a red light" at the same time your light is about to turn green. While the driver is speeding through a red light, you are safely still waiting for your green light.

PARK IT, BUDDY!

With so many people living and working in a city, sometimes owning and driving your own vehicle can be pretty frustrating. Crowded streets and limited parking are real problems drivers face. And it's also incredibly expensive to park a car in the city. In New York City, for example, you could pay as much as $225,000 to buy a parking space in an upscale neighborhood—and then have to pay a fee every year on top of that! Parking spots are in such demand that people have to get on long waiting lists to try to get one.

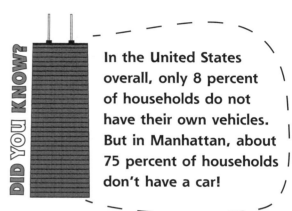

DID YOU KNOW?

In the United States overall, only 8 percent of households do not have their own vehicles. But in Manhattan, about 75 percent of households don't have a car!

To figure out how to fit more cars into small spaces, some cities have made automated garages, where elevators take your car to its spot. Because it's more compact (imagine an apartment building for cars), it can fit about three times the amount of cars as a traditional parking lot.

One alternative in many cities is to take advantage of a shared bike system. Boston, Massachusetts, has thousands of bikes in the Hubway program. They are available all day and night at hundreds of stations around the city. Riders can view a map of the service area and pay to unlock bikes they can use to ride to the station of their choice, then return the bikes there.

BETWEEN BIKES, BUSES, SUBWAYS, AND OF COURSE WALKING, MOST RESIDENTS AND VISITORS IN CITIES NEVER HAVE TO EVEN BOTHER DRIVING OR PARKING.

PEOPLE VERSUS CARS

Vehicles aren't the only motion on city streets. People on foot, called pedestrians, are also part of city traffic. And they've got to stay safe, too! Pedestrians even have their own traffic signals. When all of the cars at an intersection have red lights, pedestrians are signaled that it's safe for them to cross the street.

Sidewalks were created to run alongside roads, giving pedestrians a safe place to walk. In some cities, sidewalks are also a place where musicians, chess players, and restaurant tables can be found.

SIDEWALKS THAT ARE TOO CROWDED AND BUSY CAN CAUSE PROBLEMS.

Sidewalks are an important part of a busy city, where pedestrians can both travel and be a part of a vibrant culture. As a city planner, how would you design sidewalks to make them safe and fun?

City planners measure the amount of pedestrian traffic on a sidewalk and make corrections if they need to. **There are several levels of pedestrian traffic.**

A: At this level, people can walk freely at any speed, without bumping into anyone or having to change paths.

B: People can still walk freely, but they have to look ahead and avoid other pedestrians' paths.

C: There's still enough room to walk normally without bumping into anyone, but it's more likely people will have to avoid each other's paths.

D: People are not able to move as fast as they like because it's too crowded, and people have to avoid each other.

E: This is a crowded sidewalk. People cannot walk quickly or pass by each other easily.

DID YOU KNOW?

The Shibuya Crossing in Tokyo, Japan, is the busiest intersection in the world. Each day, 2.5 million people cross there! Crossing on foot with thousands of other people is called the "Shibuya Shuffle."

F: This level is like waiting in line at a major sporting or entertainment event. People mostly stand still or shuffle slowly as a group.

Naturally, city planners want to avoid the last few pedestrian traffic levels listed. Some changes they can make to help avoid these levels include widening the sidewalk or adjusting the timing on the street-crossing signals. If pedestrian patterns are too crowded, city planners will sometimes build bridges for vehicles over the streets so that the street can be used just for pedestrians. That way, people can walk safely without interrupting road traffic.

WALK THIS WAY

For people who can't see, finding their way around a bustling city is more difficult. But with Accessible Pedestrian Signals (APS), people who are blind

or can't see well can feel a bit safer when crossing busy streets.

With many signal systems, a loud beeping that sounds like a bird chirping starts when pedestrians are signaled to cross the street. This is for the people who can't see the signal. They hear the beeping and know it's safe for them to cross.

But sometimes it's hard to remember what each sound means, and if there's a lot of traffic noise, it can be hard to tell where the sound is coming from. If people who can't see are waiting at a busy intersection, they could miss their signal or worse: They could hear the "Walk" signal from another street and think it's for them.

New APS systems were developed to help make things safer. They now have a button with a raised arrow pointing in the direction of the street-crossing, so people can feel which street the button is for. When it's safe to cross, the button vibrates and then tells people—in words, not bird chirps!—when and for how long it's safe to cross.

DID YOU KNOW?

Most streets in Japan don't have names. Instead, entire blocks are given numbers.

MAKE YOUR OWN
SIDEWALK BRICK-LAYING PATTERN

Bricks are usually laid in straight rows, alternating slightly with each row. But sidewalk designers who want to beautify their city create different patterns for laying bricks. They use patterns that can repeat endlessly, called tessellations. A bee's honeycomb is an example of a tessellation in nature. Test your own skills and create a unique pattern for a sidewalk.

SUPPLIES

- ☑ 4 x 4 inch piece of card stock or light cardboard (it must be square to work, so measure the sides carefully)
- ☑ pencil or something to write with
- ☑ ruler or straight edge
- ☑ scissors
- ☑ tape
- ☑ large piece of poster board
- ☑ different-colored markers

1 Label each corner of your square clockwise, starting in the upper left corner: A, B, C, and D.

2 On your square, draw a curved or zigzag line right down the middle from top to bottom. Keep it simple, don't make your line too curvy or too zigzagged.

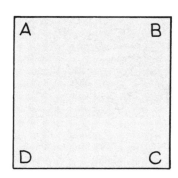

3 Draw another line from left to right. Again, keep it simple. Cut along the lines so you have four pieces.

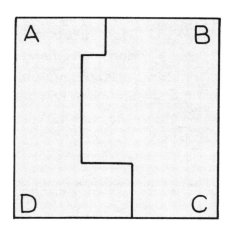
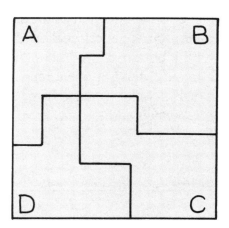

4 On a flat surface, line up the pieces so all the right angles (the corners with the letters) all meet in the center. The letters should read clockwise, starting in the upper left: C, D, A B.

5 Tape all your pieces together. This is your stencil.

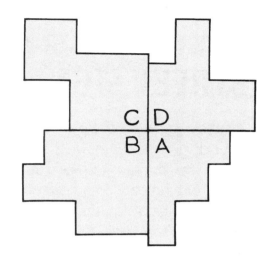

6 Lay the stencil on your poster board along the top edge and trace around it with your pencil. Then slide the stencil over and line up the edges of the stencil with the edge you just drew. It will fit together like a puzzle piece. Trace the stencil again. Keep sliding the stencil over and tracing it until you run out of room. Then drop the stencil down, lining up the matching edge again. Trace another row.

7 Continue tracing until your poster board is filled. Color your pieces with markers, either alternating colors or in any pattern you like. Your "sidewalk" is complete!

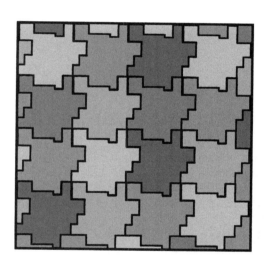

DID YOU KNOW?

Rio de Janeiro in Brazil is famous for its black-and-white mosaic sidewalk patterns—each beach walk has a different pattern. But in 2013, the city added an update: It embedded special barcodes called QR codes that people can scan with their smartphones to get travel tips and historic information!

DESIGN YOUR OWN
STREET SIGN

SUPPLIES

- ☑ card stock, white construction paper, or poster board
- ☑ pencil and eraser
- ☑ different-colored markers

Imagine you are a city planner. There's a problem on one of your city's streets: A new school opened on Smart Street, one of the smaller roads off Main Street. Now, during weekdays, traffic turning onto Smart Street is backing up onto Main Street. Design a sign that clearly tells drivers they can't turn left onto Smart Street during school hours on weekdays. Instead, they can drive one more block and take Easy Street.

1 Brainstorm what kind of sign would be most effective to help direct the flow of traffic. It should be clear so that every driver understands what it means. Some things to keep in mind:

* **Color:** What color will be most visible to drivers, but not look too much like an existing sign? For example, a red sign might make people stop.

* **Shape:** Certain shapes are used for different types of signs, such as the octagon for stop signs and the triangle for yield signs.

* **Words:** Any letters should be easy to read. Drivers don't have a lot of time to read, so try not to write long sentences. Keep it clear and to the point!

2 Draw your sign onto your card stock or poster board in pencil first. Once you're happy with your design, start drawing with markers.

3 Show your sign to friends or family, describing the problem in your city. See if they understand your sign. If they come up with good ideas, you can make a new sign that would direct traffic even better.

Try This! Design a sign to fix a problem in the town or city that you live in. Is there a place where traffic is always jammed? Where people often get confused about directions, or pedestrians have trouble crossing the street? What kind of signs would help these areas work better?

CHAPTER 6
Getting Around Underground

Have you ever ridden on the subway? How does underground transportation work and why do people choose to use it? This is a way to get around cities that avoids all of the busy street traffic.

EACH MAJOR CITY HAS A **UNIQUE** NAME FOR ITS UNDERGROUND TRANSPORTATION SYSTEM.

In Washington, DC, it's called the Metro. People in Boston call their subway system the T. In London, it's called the Tube. Despite the different names, they're all the same basic thing—an underground railway system that transports people all over the city. These subways are a type of **rapid transit**.

HEADING UNDERGROUND

Words to know!

unique: special or unusual.

rapid transit: a transportation system that moves a lot of people around a city quickly and smoothly.

tunnel: an underground passageway that goes through or under natural or manmade obstacles such as rivers, mountains, roads, and buildings.

By the mid-1800s, the population of London had grown so much that something had to be done about the crowds of people moving throughout the city. The idea of an underground railway system was born.

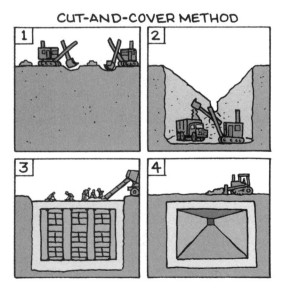

CUT-AND-COVER METHOD

The first **tunnels** were built using a cut-and-cover method. This involved digging a huge hole large enough to fit the train and station. Then walls and a roof were built inside the hole, forming a tunnel. The roof was built strong enough to hold the dirt and anything else put on top of it, such as roads and buildings. Finally, the trench was filled with dirt, hiding the new subway tunnel underneath.

While this method was effective and relatively safe, it completely tore up the streets above the tunnel. The area was unusable during the **excavation** and building of the tunnels. This inconvenienced a lot of people.

After the first tunnels were built, engineers developed a new process called the tunneling shield method. This let laborers dig out the tunnel while surrounded by a temporary protective barrier. With this system, builders could construct the support walls while they were excavating the tunnel. This also meant that most of the ground surface didn't have to be broken during construction.

Words to know!

excavation: making a trench or tunnel by digging.

mechanical: done by machine, not by a person.

conveyor: a moving belt that carries objects from one place to another.

debris: the scattered pieces of something that has been broken or destroyed.

bedrock: the solid rock earth, well beneath the softer surface of soil, sand, clay, gravel, or water.

TUNNELING SHIELD METHOD

Today, a tunnel-boring machine does the work. This massive machine is like an enormous **mechanical** mole digging through the earth. On the front of the machine are discs and scrapers that crush rocks and dirt. Then a **conveyor** hauls away the **debris** to clear the tunnel space. This mechanical giant plows through even the most solid underground areas, such as **bedrock**.

Words to know!

pollutant: waste material that damages the environment.

steam-powered: powered by an engine that burns wood or coal to heat water and create steam.

ventilation shaft: a tunnel or passage that brings in fresh air.

third rail: the source of power for electric subway systems; a brush, wheel, or sliding "shoe" touches the rail and sends power to the train's electric motor.

DID YOU KNOW?

Old New York City subway cars that can't be used anymore are stripped of **pollutants** and materials that have any value. Then they are sunk in the ocean off the Atlantic Coast to create artificial reefs for fish.

The first trains to run in underground tunnels were **steam-powered** trains. **Ventilation shafts** built along the tunnel allowed the steam to escape and fresh air to enter.

Very soon after subways systems started, though, trains began running on electricity. Overhead wires or a special rail called the **third rail** supply power to the trains.

WHO'S DRIVING?

In many subway systems, specially trained people drive the trains. There's usually an operator in the front train who controls the speed, including stops and starts. The conductor rides in the middle of the train. This person makes announcements to the passengers and makes sure the train is lined up properly at the stations so passengers can safely get on and off.

Other systems are automated. This means that computers control the train, even though each train is still closely watched by people in a control room connected by cameras. The computers can even tell if there's anything dangerous on the tracks. People in the control room can talk to passengers with a two-way radio system.

SAFETY FIRST

The first priority of any system is the safety of its riders and workers. That's why subway systems use **track geometry cars**. These are train cars that run all over the subway system measuring the conditions of the tunnels. Because subway systems can be damaged by everyday use, just like the roads above them, track geometry cars are equipped with technology that lets them measure any changes in the underground system. **They look for a number of changes.**

- Alignment, which is how straight the tracks are.

- Curvature, to make sure the track isn't curving any more or less than it was designed to do.

- Rail gauge, which is the distance between the rails.

- Track temperature. Debris on the track can heat up from friction and cause a fire. The geometry cars measure the temperature and take care of any hot spots.

- Clearance from the station platforms and overhead materials, to make sure there's still the proper spacing for the train.

Words to know!

track geometry car: the vehicle that runs on subway systems to monitor the conditions of the system and report if anything needs to be fixed or repaired.

TO MAKE SURE EVERYTHING IS RUNNING SMOOTHLY AND SAFELY, COMPUTER SYSTEMS KEEP TRACK OF EVERY TRAIN'S LOCATION.

THE MODERN UNDERGROUND

Subway systems never stop changing. Improvements for safety and efficiency are always being made. In New York City, some subway cars now have free wireless Internet for riders. A company in Barcelona, Spain, developed technology to scan subway cars and tell waiting riders which parts of the train have the most available seats. They can also tell which car is best if they need wheelchair access.

DID YOU KNOW?

New York City's subway has more stations than any other in the world. There are 468 places to get on and off.

GOING UNDER!

For travelers going between the cities of London and Paris, the English Channel—ranging in width from around 20 to 150 miles (33 to 240 kilometers) wide—was a big obstacle. As early as 1802, a tunnel was proposed to cross the waters. Back then, plans included oil lamps, horse-drawn coaches, and an artificial island in the middle for changing horses!

Since an underwater passage would make crossing the channel so much easier than boats or ferries, the French and English governments discussed building the tunnel for decades. Construction finally began in 1988. The tunnel was opened in 1994. Called the "Chunnel" (a combination of "Channel" and "Tunnel"), the tunnel is about 31 miles (50.5 kilometers) long, with the longest undersea portion of any tunnel in the world. High-speed trains carry passengers across the channel. The ride connects the cities of London to Paris, and it takes passengers two hours and 15 minutes to make the trip.

Saving electricity is another improvement being made to subways. To accelerate from a station, a train full of passengers uses as much power as 1,000 homes in the United States for 30 seconds. But just a few seconds later, that energy is lost when the train puts on the brakes at the next stop. Even with the amount of power a train loses coming into a station, it still takes about 27 percent less energy for people to ride the train than to drive. To save even more energy, engineers have tried strategies such as building an incline on the approach to a platform and a downhill slope away from it.

DID YOU KNOW?

The Pyongyang Metro in North Korea plays patriotic anthems over the speaker system for riders to listen to.

ENGINEERS ARE ALWAYS TRYING TO THINK OF NEW DESIGNS TO HELP SAVE ELECTRICITY.

DOWN UNDER

The subway isn't the only part of the city's infrastructure that's hidden under your feet. Cables for electricity and telephones and supply lines for gas and water all can be run underground.

There's a benefit to running them underground instead of above ground. Underground cables and supply lines don't interfere with buildings, trees, or transportation such as overhead lines sometimes can. They're also less affected by bad weather—fallen tree limbs don't break underground wires or pipes. They also are hidden, so they don't make the scenery look unattractive!

There are some downsides, though. It costs more for cables and pipes to be run underground, since digging or drilling through rock takes more time and money than just stringing them up overhead. And it's sometimes harder to fix breaks underground, too.

MAKE YOUR OWN
SUBWAY SYSTEM CROSS-SECTION MODEL

What happens beneath the streets is as fascinating and busy as what goes on above. With this project, you will create a cut-away of the amazing world beneath a city to see what it looks like underground.

1 Position the foam rectangle so it's tall, like a tower. Cut a piece of black construction paper and attach it to the top of the tower. This will be the road surface. You can draw stripes on the road or even attach a bench or street sign.

2 About a half inch (1 centimeter) below the road surface, push a straw through the foam so it goes in one side and out the other. Run a piece of yarn or string through the straw and use your markers to label the straw "telephone cable." If you don't have enough room to write that, put a number beside the straw, then make a note of what that number means (1=telephone cable) with your pencil and paper.

3 About a half inch (1 centimeter) below your telephone cable, push another straw through. Thread a different-colored yarn through the straw. Label this straw "electric cable."

4 About 1 inch (2½ centimeters) below the electricity cable, push a wider straw or tube through. Label this one "water supply pipe."

DID YOU KNOW?

Underground systems need fresh air constantly brought into the tunnels. Fans and air shafts push and pull fresh air into the tunnels for people to breathe.

SUPPLIES

- ☑ long foam rectangle
- ☑ black construction paper
- ☑ glue
- ☑ various sizes of tubes and thin boxes, such as toothpaste boxes, straws, paper towel rolls
- ☑ pencil and paper
- ☑ yarn or string in different colors
- ☑ markers or pens

5 Another inch (2½ centimeters) lower, push another wide straw through and label it "gas supply pipe."

6 Below your gas supply pipe, push one more straw through and label it "storm drain." This is the pipe that carries away rainwater that collects off the city streets through the grates on the sides of the road.

7 About 2 inches (5 centimeters) below the storm drain, push a paper towel tube through your foam. This is your underground railway. If you want, put a train car in it! Take your marker and draw a short horizontal line next to your underground railway. Mark on the foam or on your paper legend that this is 30 feet (9 meters) below street surface.

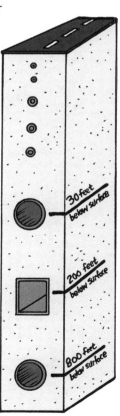

CONSTRUCTION PAPER →
← ROAD SURFACE
← TELEPHONE CABLE
← ELECTRIC CABLE
STRAW WITH YARN
← WATER SUPPLY PIPE
WIDER STRAW
← GAS SUPPLY PIPE
← STORM DRAIN PIPE
PAPER TOWEL TUBE
← UNDERGROUND RAILWAY
TOOTHPASTE BOX
← SEWER SYSTEM
PAPER TOWEL TUBE
← WATER SUPPLY SYSTEM

8 Under the subway, push a toothpaste box through. Label it "sewer system." This is the tunnel that carries away dirty wastewater. Draw a horizontal line beside your sewer pipe. Label this as 200 feet (61 meters) below the surface.

9 Finally, underneath the sewer system, push through one last paper towel tube for the water supply system. This brings freshwater into the city for drinking and other uses. Make a horizontal mark beside your deep water supply. This is 800 feet (244 meters) below the surface.

Try This! Think about why each system is at each level. Try switching around the levels of some of the systems on a new piece of foam. What problems would be caused by the water supply switching with the underground railway? Would it be better or worse if the telephone cables were below the sewage system? Try different orders to see if the system we have makes the most sense.

30 feet below surface

200 feet below surface

800 feet below surface

CHAPTER 7
Urbanization

Do you think most people in the United States live in urban or rural areas? The answer to this question might surprise you. According to the United States **Census Bureau**, the 2010 census showed that 80 percent of Americans live in urban areas.

California is the most urban state, with 95 percent of the population living in cities. Maine and Vermont are the least urban states, with less than 40 percent of their populations living in cities. Charlotte, North Carolina, Austin, Texas, and Las Vegas, Nevada, are the fastest-growing cities in the country.

Some cities, such as Los Angeles, keep spreading out, creating a bigger and bigger **metropolitan** area. But other cities, such as New York City, can't spread out because they're bordered by rivers, oceans, or other natural boundaries. So as the population of New York City grows, it means that more and more people are living in the same amount of space. As a city planner, how would you make sure your city grows in a way that meets the needs of all the people who want to live there?

Words to know!

metropolitan: describes a city and its surrounding area.

ELBOW ROOM

Have you ever shared your bedroom with a brother or sister? Sometimes it's fun and sometimes it's crowded. Imagine sharing your bedroom with three other people. Or four. Or more!

In overcrowded buildings, there is very little personal space and no privacy. Sometimes buildings that house too many people can be very dirty.

DID YOU KNOW?

The most densely populated city in the world is Manila in the Philippines. There are more than 111,000 people per square mile. That's one person for about every 250 square feet (23 square meters).

When a city has too many overcrowded buildings, the schools, food supply system, water system, transportation, and other **infrastructures** can suffer. Overcrowded conditions can make people unhappy. It helps when crowded city areas have public places where kids can hang out or play sports. Lots of cities have parks and green areas where residents can go to relax and get some fresh air in the open space.

Some countries and cities have resorted to dramatic attempts to ease overcrowding. In China, sometimes families pay a fine if they have more than one child.

Words to know!

infrastructure: the large-scale public systems, services, and facilities of a country or region, including power and water supplies, public transportation, telecommunications, roads, and schools.

FEEDING A CITY

There are more than 8 million people in New York City. If everyone ate a healthy diet, each person would consume more than a ton of food per year! But even if all of the food production in New York State went to the city, it would only feed 55 percent of the city's population. The rest of the city—and the rest of the state—would have nothing.

Even if the city could live off the food produced by New York State alone, production would drop in the winter, when cold weather stops most crops from growing. Shipping food from warmer climates is the only way a city like New York City can feed everyone year round.

IS IT HOT IN HERE?

What did New York City look like before it was New York City? It was covered in forests and teeming with **wildlife**. It's hard to imagine now, but cities used to be pieces of **undeveloped** land with very little impact from humans. When cities are built, the natural **landscape** is dramatically changed or completely destroyed. But there are also changes that you can't see.

Words to know!

wildlife: animals, birds, and other things that live wild in nature.

undeveloped: not built on or changed.

landscape: a large area of land with specific features.

urban heat island: a dense cityscape that raises the temperature in the surrounding area.

CITIES ACTUALLY RAISE THE AIR TEMPERATURE!

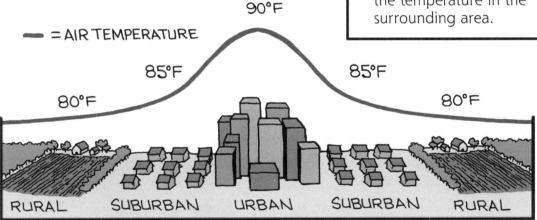

= AIR TEMPERATURE

90°F
85°F   85°F
80°F   80°F

RURAL   SUBURBAN   URBAN   SUBURBAN   RURAL

Cities can cause an **urban heat island**. The air temperature of a city with more than 1 million people is warmer than its surroundings. Cities are usually around 2 to 5 degrees Fahrenheit (1 to 2.5 degrees Celsius) warmer, but they can get as much as 22 degrees Fahrenheit (12 degrees Celsius) warmer!

These urban heat islands happen because cities do not have enough natural **vegetation** and open land to absorb water and heat. Hard city surfaces such as asphalt, concrete, glass, and steel heat up, and they release the heat back into the surroundings.

How would you keep your city from getting too hot? People can take steps by planting more trees and vegetation along city streets and creating "green" roofs. These rooftop gardens absorb rain and heat from the sun, helping buildings to stay cooler. There are also new pavements that are made of materials that reflect heat and stay cool.

Words to know!

vegetation: all the plant life in a particular area.

infrared: a kind of image that shows how hot (or cool) its subject is.

urban decay: when a city or part of a city is neglected or virtually abandoned.

Infrared photos of New York City show that areas with trees and vegetation—as in Central Park—have cooler air temperatures than the surrounding city streets.

GONE AWAY

While the populations of most cities are rising, shrinking populations can also cause problems. **Urban decay** happens when part of a city, big or small, is neglected to the point that the area falls into disrepair and is abandoned by its residents.

There are many causes of urban decay. Highway construction can make an area more difficult to access. If people no longer go to the stores there, they might close or move. Sometimes people leave to live in more desirable areas. Other times new laws limit development, so the government stops spending money in an area. When the residents are too poor to keep improving and maintaining the neighborhood themselves, the whole area suffers.

The "Rust Belt" is a nickname for the **postindustrial** areas suffering from urban decay that span from central New York to eastern Wisconsin. This area used to contain most of America's **manufacturing industry**. As factory jobs became automated, fewer workers were needed. Over time, factories moved to other countries with lower manufacturing costs. With no jobs to work at, residents left and the area experienced a long period of urban decay.

Improvement after urban decay is possible. **Urban renewal** happens when local governments or groups of concerned citizens work together to bring an area back. These groups build community parks, repair buildings, and provide funding to struggling residents who otherwise might be forced to move to another part of town. With so many people moving into urban areas, it makes sense to renew the areas that already exist.

The city of Pittsburgh, Pennsylvania, is an example of a successful urban renewal. During the **Industrial Revolution**, the city thrived, but after that the city became run-down and people left for other places. In the 1950s, the city began a big urban renewal program downtown, demolishing old buildings to build modern office towers, a sports arena, and public parks. It worked—and downtown became a hot new riverfront location for residents.

Words to know!

postindustrial: describes an area formerly used for manufacturing.

manufacturing industry: the production of large quantities of products, usually in a factory.

urban renewal: the development of urban areas that have become run down, by renovating old buildings or building new ones.

Industrial Revolution: a time of far-reaching change when the large-scale production of goods began.

ABANDONED CITIES

Sometimes cities full of activity and residents quickly become abandoned. These cities are called ghost towns because the city still has buildings and sidewalks and streetlights, but no people living there.

Earthquakes or other natural disasters can damage or destroy entire cities, and residents don't want to rebuild their homes and businesses in the unsafe areas. In Centralia, Pennsylvania, the situation was a little different. Established in 1866, Centralia was populated by the people who worked in its coal mines. But in 1962, a part of the coal mine beneath the town was accidentally set on fire. Like a river the fire spread beneath the ground through the other coal deposits and veins. For years, city workers tried to extinguish the fire by digging trenches or pouring in water.

But after almost 20 years, the fire still burned. When a 12-year-old boy was almost swallowed by a **sinkhole** filled with poisonous **carbon monoxide**, it was the last straw for the residents. In 1982, the city's residents relocated, leaving Centralia abandoned. Traffic was detoured around the city and plants grew over the unused roads. Most buildings eventually caught fire or were leveled to prevent fires.

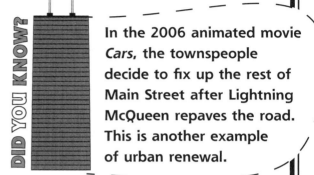

DID YOU KNOW?

In the 2006 animated movie *Cars*, the townspeople decide to fix up the rest of Main Street after Lightning McQueen repaves the road. This is another example of urban renewal.

Words to know!

sinkhole: a hole or depression in the land that opens up suddenly.

carbon monoxide: a poisonous gas produced by burning fossil fuels such as gasoline.

EXPERIMENT WITH POPULATION GROWTH

Why is overcrowding such a problem for city residents? This project shows the effect of overcrowding on living things.

SUPPLIES

- ☑ planting pots or recycled containers
- ☑ potting soil
- ☑ quick-growing plant seeds such as radish or beans
- ☑ water
- ☑ paper and pencil

1 Fill your containers about three-quarters full of potting soil. Press the soil down lightly, but don't pack it too tightly.

2 Look at the directions on the package of seeds. In the first pot, plant exactly the number of seeds recommended by the package directions. In the second pot, plant five times the number of recommended seeds. Record the number of seeds you planted in each pot.

3 Cover the seeds in both pots with a layer of potting soil. Gently water both pots according to the package directions. Over the next few days, treat both pots exactly the same—give them the same temperature conditions and amounts of sun and water.

4 When the seeds have fully sprouted, count the sprouts in each pot. On your paper next to the number of seeds you planted in each pot, record how many sprouts and their condition. Are they the same height in both pots? The same color? What other differences do you notice? What conclusions can you draw from your observations?

Try This! Let the seedlings grow and then look at the quality of the vegetables that are produced. What's different about them? Calculate the percentage of good vegetables from each pot. This will help you to better understand the effects of too much overcrowding on the seeds.

MAKE YOUR OWN
CITY GROWTH OVERLAY

SUPPLIES

- ☑ poster board
- ☑ pencil and other things to write and draw with
- ☑ clear sheet protectors or transparencies
- ☑ tape

You often can't find actual photos or images of a city from when it was first built and populated. With this project, you will simulate what the changes in a city must have looked like over time.

1 Start with your poster board. Imagine it's the early 1800s and you're looking from the edge of a big lake at a settlement that will eventually become a city. What do you see? Maybe a few scattered homes and a lot of trees. Maybe a trader is paddling his canoe toward the shore. There might be a stream flowing through the land to the lake.

2 Use your pencil to draw the undeveloped land and the small community on your poster board.

3 Now take one of your transparency pages and lay it over your entire scene. Tape it into place at the top so you can flip it up. Imagine what the scene might look like in the late 1800s. The population will have grown to hundreds of thousands of people. There will be grid-patterned streets now. Small buildings fill city blocks. Instead of traders in canoes there are now steamboats.

4 On the transparency paper, draw over your first picture with all of the features you've just imagined. Your city could be growing outward and getting denser.

The city of Sitka, Alaska, is the largest city in the United States in terms of land area, with 2,870 square miles (267 square meters). That's more than twice the size of the state of Rhode Island.

5 Lay one more transparency over your project and tape it in place. Picture the city as it looks today. The street grid is still there, but now many buildings in the city center are replaced by skyscrapers. Maybe a few blocks of the small buildings have been replaced with a park. There might be tourist cruise boats on the water.

6 Draw over your picture on the new piece of transparency.

7 When you're finished, you can label each of the layers, then flip through them to see the change in the city over the years.

Try This! Add a fourth layer and label it "future." Decide how far into the future you want to imagine and draw more changes to the city. What is there more of and what is there less of? Use your knowledge of urban decay and urban renewal to guess how areas of your city will develop.

MAKE YOUR OWN
CITY GROWTH FLIP BOOK

SUPPLIES

- ☑ several sheets of white paper
- ☑ scissors
- ☑ stapler
- ☑ something to draw with (start with pencil, then color over it)

Here's another way to show city growth. With the previous project, you saw how cities change over time. But how does urbanization look up close? With this project, you can draw the progress of a building as it changes over time.

1 Cut the sheets of paper into at least 10 rectangles, 6 by 3 inches (15 by 7.5 centimeters) each. These will be your flip book pages.

2 Stack the pages neatly on top of each other. Carefully slide the pages over to the left just a tiny bit. You want each far right edge of a page to extend just a tiny bit farther than the page above it, kind of like a fan. This will make flipping the pages easier.

STAPLE HERE

FAN THE PAGES

3 Staple the left edge of the pages together. Since they're spread out a little, don't staple too close to the very left edge or you'll miss a few pages.

4 On the first page, draw the first stage of your building. Keep it simple—maybe just a bumpy line that's a dirt road with a small building on top.

5 Now take another small piece of paper, one that's not stapled into your pile. This is going to be your stencil. Lay it over your first drawing and trace that drawing on your stencil.

6 Turn to the next page in your book. Lay the stencil under this second page, so it shows through. Lightly trace your first drawing onto the second page. Now draw something new on the second page, like a second story on your building.

7 Take the stencil out from under the second page, place it on top of the second page, and trace the new drawing onto your stencil. Now the stencil shows the change in the building.

8 Turn to the third page, and repeat the process. First, trace the stencil onto your blank third page. Then add something new to the third page drawing. Finally, trace the new addition onto your growing stencil.

9 Keep repeating until your book is full. When you flip through the pages, you'll see your building grow and change over time. **Here are some ideas:**

* The building can grow to be a skyscraper;

* The road can change from dirt to asphalt;

* The building can experience urban renewal when it's "reborn" as a community center or turned into a green park;

* Other buildings can grow up around your building;

* The building can begin to experience urban decay, crumbling down or having broken windows. To demolish your building, erase parts of your stencil as you move it through the book.

Try This! Make more flip books showing different areas of a city. Try showing how a park or a street corner would develop over time. Keep in mind that city areas can change a lot. What was once a building could now be a community garden. Be creative with how your areas change! Think about the pros and cons of living in a big city. What makes a city a wonderful place and what makes it a more challenging place? How can city planners help a city change for the better?

CHAPTER 8
Who's in Charge?

How are all of the roads, power grids, sewers, subways, and other parts of a city's infrastructure maintained? If you look around, you'll see that a lot of the people on a city's streets are working. Road workers might be repairing a big pothole in the street or street cleaners might be cleaning the streets. Sanitation workers are taking away everyone's trash and recycling. Police officers are on patrol to keep the streets safe.

Other workers could be in a park, running an after-school program for kids or doing jobs such as air pollution inspectors, health department workers, secretaries, and firefighters. These are all city workers, people who work for the city's local government. Along with workers who labor for the city, there are elected officials. These people work as a group to make the laws that govern the city.

LET'S MAKE IT OFFICIAL

In the United States, the **federal** government makes laws that apply to the entire country. Individual states make laws that apply to each state. Every city or town also makes its own set of laws. A city's government is called a **municipal** government or local government. The elected officials who work for the municipal government serve the city's residents.

The municipal government provides the services that maintain all of the parts of the city.

While the governor is the head of the state's government, the **mayor** is the head of the city's government. Some municipal governments are divided into **councils** that are in charge of specific types of issues. Others are divided into several branches that each has different divisions within it.

Words to know!

federal: the national government of a country.

municipal: having to do with a city's activities or management.

mayor: the elected official in charge of a city's government.

council: a group of elected officials.

DID YOU KNOW?

At age 11, Brian Zimmerman was elected mayor of the town of Crabb, Texas. The title was honorary because the town wasn't incorporated, meaning it didn't have an official municipal government.

CITIES

The local government is usually divided up in a way similar to the federal government.

- **Legislative branch** makes the laws in the community;

- **Executive branch** controls the community's money and approves or **vetoes** laws;

- **Judicial branch** handles legal issues in the community and upholds the laws;

- **Administrative branch** provides oversight of all city departments on behalf of a council or mayor.

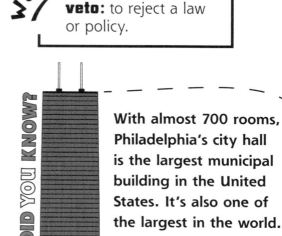

Words to know!

veto: to reject a law or policy.

DID YOU KNOW?

With almost 700 rooms, Philadelphia's city hall is the largest municipal building in the United States. It's also one of the largest in the world.

In most communities, a council is in charge of the legislative branch, the mayor is in charge of the executive branch, and the city manager is in charge of the administrative branch. The city clerk often leads the judicial branch.

CITY HALL

This is not the structure in every city around the world, though. Sometimes the structures are similar to this, but have different names for each branch and position.

For example, sometimes a city manager is in charge of everyone below him or her in the city. But in other systems, the city manager position doesn't exist and the mayor is the city's chief executive.

MAYORS IN DIFFERENT CITIES HAVE DIFFERENT RESPONSIBILITIES DEPENDING ON THE WAY THE GOVERNMENT IS STRUCTURED.

Below are two examples of government structures with different roles for the mayor.

Council-manager government: A city council rules over the legislative branch. The mayor's role is equal to those of the other council members. The city manager handles the administration of the government.

Mayor-council government: The mayor's position is separate from the city council. In this structure, the mayor is in charge of the executive branch while the council is in charge of the legislative branch.

Mayors in mayor-council governments are not all the same. They can be "strong mayors," meaning they have a lot of executive power. They can also be "weak mayors," meaning they can do nothing without the council's approval.

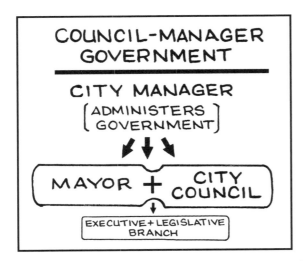

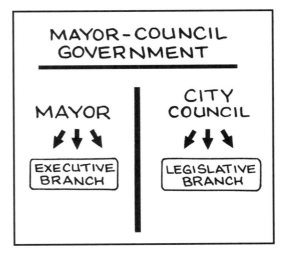

MAKE YOUR OWN
MAYOR FOR A DAY MAZE

With so much involved in overseeing a city, mayors have lots of daily responsibilities. In this project, you will find your way through a day in the life of a mayor while avoiding pitfalls.

1 Cut the cardboard cereal box into long, thin strips, each 1½ inches (about 4 centimeters) wide.

2 Bend ½ inch (1¼ centimeters) of each strip lengthwise. Make the creases sharp. Each strip should now look like a bench with a very narrow seat. These will be the walls of your maze.

3 With the pencil, sketch out your maze in the shoebox lid. Make sure the spaces between the maze walls are wide enough for a marble to roll through without getting stuck. There should be a start and an end. Add two dead ends to represent pitfalls in your mayor's day. Label what these problems might be.

4 Once your maze layout is complete, tape the short folded edges of the cardboard strips into the shoebox lid along the lines you drew. Make sure the strips stand up straight so they make walls. They should be about 1 inch (about 2.5 centimeters) high.

5 Use the scissors to cut two holes in the base at the "dead ends" of your maze paths. These should be large enough for the marble to pass through so it falls out at the dead end.

6 Put your marble at the start. Try to guide the marble through the maze by tipping and tilting the box top—but watch out for the holes leading to the dead ends! Start over if you fall through. When you make it to the end of the maze, congratulations! You've successfully made it through one day as a mayor.

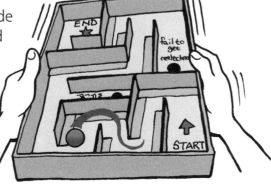

Try This! Try completing the maze again. This time, if you fall through a hole, try to come up with a solution to the problem before you start again. How would you respond to a repair crew failing to fix a pothole? How about not getting re-elected? You can also change the labels on the pitfalls so that you can come up with solutions to many problems. You may have to redesign your maze if you get too good at it!

FAVORITE SON

Some mayors go above and beyond the normal duties of their office. Mayor Cory Booker of Newark, New Jersey, who was elected in 2006, gets a lot of attention for the things he does outside the office.

Before he was elected mayor, Booker went on a 10-day hunger strike while living in a tent to protest the problems of drug dealing and violence in the city. In 2010, Booker and other volunteers shoveled an elderly man's driveway after the man's daughter asked for Booker's help on **Twitter**.

Continuing his streak of good deeds, Booker once saved a woman from a house fire. He suffered smoke inhalation and second-degree burns on his hands, but most likely saved the woman's life. Mayor Booker also rescued a dog from the freezing cold. He spotted the shivering dog while driving and brought it to safety. In 2012, he chose to live on a food budget of $30 a week to call attention to the struggles of Americans who survive only on food purchased with **food stamps**.

After Hurricane Sandy caused major power outages in New York and New Jersey, he opened his home to residents who were without power.

Words to know!

Twitter: an online service that allows users to send and read messages called tweets. Tweets are limited to 140 characters.

food stamps: the common name for a program officially called the Supplemental Nutrition Assistance Program. This government program gives low-income people a debit card they can use in stores to buy food.

WRITE A LETTER FOR COMMUNITY INVOLVEMENT

The city government works for its people and always likes to get ideas and feedback from residents and visitors. Even if you don't live in a city, your government needs input from you and others in your community to keep improving the place you live. When you write a letter to your city's or town's elected officials, you're showing them you care about your community.

1 Is there a situation in your community you're concerned about? Maybe you've heard something on the news that doesn't sound right. Or maybe there's an intersection that's dangerous to cross on your bike. Think about something that you think needs to change in your community.

2 Now think about a possible solution to the problem. If it's a busy intersection, you could suggest putting in new signs to warn drivers that kids are crossing. Maybe the intersection needs a crossing signal. Your city officials might not use your suggestions, but giving them ideas shows them that you care, and also might help them find their own solutions.

3 Working with an adult, find out to whom you should address your concern. Should you write to the mayor? If your idea is about a small change, maybe you should send your letter to the head of a department.

4 Write your letter to the person you have chosen. Start by telling him or her who you are. Then write about your concern and how the problem has affected you. Explain why correcting this problem would help the entire community. Then list your solutions to the problem. End your letter by thanking the official for his or her work in your community and signing: "Sincerely, (your name)."

5 Mail your letter! Keep in mind that while one voice can get attention, sometimes it takes a bigger effort to cause a change. Your letter is just a start. If you're passionate about the problem, stick with it! What more can you do?

Try This! Find out when the next town or city meeting is scheduled. If you attend, you can find out more about the problems in your town and what's being done to solve them. Maybe your concern has started a conversation about solutions in your town meeting!

DID YOU KNOW?

Hilmar Moore was the mayor of Richmond, Texas, for 63 years!

TEAMWORK

Even though they're divided up differently, all municipal governments work to take the best possible care of their cities. They're not alone in their work. Other government agencies in a city take care of certain services.

- **Fire Department:** maintains fire safety in the community, putting out fires and making sure buildings are safe.

- **Police Department:** upholds the laws and protects citizens.

- **Health Department:** makes sure all businesses, hospitals, schools, and other community resources follow certain rules to keep everyone healthy and safe.

- **Sanitation Department:** disposes of garbage and coordinates recycling programs.

- **Public Works:** fixes damaged roads, puts up traffic signs, and maintains road surfaces.

CHAPTER 9

Cities and Nature

Do you like to play outside? If you live in a city, you know how important playgrounds and parks are, because they give kids a place to run around. You've learned that cities raise the air temperature around them and that increasing the amount of trees and vegetation in the city helps lower the temperature.

Plants even improve the quality of the air. But with so much land used by streets and buildings, can cities really share space with nature? How do people add green space to a concrete **environment**?

ARE THERE OTHER WAYS WE CAN REDUCE THE IMPACT THAT CITIES MAKE ON OUR ENVIRONMENT?

CHAIN REACTION

Millions of years ago, a Tyrannosaurus rex died in a swamp. Her body, along with the ferns and other plants surrounding her, **decayed**. They were buried by new plant growth, and their **organic** materials were slowly absorbed into the earth. Over time, because of changes in the environment and shifting landscape, the dinosaur and plant remains were buried deep in the earth.

Over millions of years, the pressure of the earth above them turned the dinosaur remains combined with the remains of plants and other animals into oil, coal, and natural gas. These substances are known as **fossil fuels** because they come from **fossils** of plants and animals.

> **Words to Know!**
>
> **environment:** everything in nature, living and nonliving, including animals, plants, rocks, soil, and water.
>
> **decay:** to rot.
>
> **organic:** something that is or was living, such as wood, paper, grass, and insects.
>
> **fossil fuels:** oil, natural gas, and coal, which are natural fuels that formed long ago from the remains of living organisms.
>
> **fossil:** the remains or traces of ancient plants or animals.

DID YOU KNOW?

Urban parks provide nature for city residents. Fairmount Park in Philadelphia is one of the larger municipal parks, with more than 4,000 acres. New York City's Central Park is 840 acres and is one of the most visited in the world.

During the European Industrial Revolution of the mid-1700s, humans began to use these fossil fuels. All of the factories built in urban areas during that time needed lots of power. Factories started burning fossil fuels instead of wood to power their machines. Electricity is made in many ways, but burning coal and other fossil fuels is a major source of our electricity. And, of course, most cars run on fossil fuels.

Words to know!

greenhouse gas: a gas such as water vapor, carbon dioxide, or methane that traps heat and contributes to warming temperatures.

atmosphere: the blanket of air surrounding the earth.

global warming: an increase in the average temperature of the earth's atmosphere, enough to cause climate change.

There are two problems with burning fossil fuels. First, the supply of fossil fuels is limited. Because these fuels take millions of years to form, they are used up faster than the earth can make them. Second, scientists believe burning fossil fuels creates **greenhouse gases**, which trap heat in the **atmosphere**. These gases are like a blanket around the earth that keeps heat in, making the air warmer. In this way, greenhouse gases contribute to **global warming**.

CITIES CONSUME 75 PERCENT OF THE ENERGY USED AROUND THE WORLD.

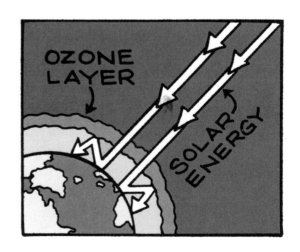

OZONE LAYER

SOLAR ENERGY

Since the start of the Industrial Revolution, burning fossil fuels has contributed to a 40-percent increase in carbon dioxide, a common greenhouse gas, in the atmosphere. With dense city populations burning lots of fossil fuels for transportation, lighting, heat, air conditioning, hot water, and other uses, it's clear why cities need to reduce the amount of fuel they use.

TAKING STEPS

In the late 1990s, a group of countries that were worried about the environmental effects of greenhouse gases joined together. They wanted to battle global warming.

These countries worked together to create an agreement called the **Kyoto Protocol**.

This international agreement between the countries is supposed to reduce the amount of greenhouse gases in the atmosphere. The main greenhouse gases are carbon dioxide, methane, and nitrous oxide. When nations signed the agreement, they committed to reducing their reported 1990 greenhouse gas emissions by around 5 percent by 2012. Some countries, such as Belgium, achieved this goal. Others, such as the Ukraine, reduced their emissions by way more than the goal amount! And some countries, such as the United States, didn't even participate.

The countries that met the goal did it in many different ways. Some used **renewable energy** sources such as solar or wind power.

Words to know!

Kyoto Protocol: the international agreement to reduce greenhouse gases around the world.

renewable energy: energy that doesn't get used up, including solar and wind.

GOING GREEN

Barcelona, Spain, began thinking green long before the Kyoto Protocol. In the mid-1800s, Spanish designer Ildefons Cerdà planned out the Eixample District to be a garden-city oasis. He designed streets that welcomed sunlight and airflow, along with squares that had gardens on every side.

Unfortunately, because of the demands on limited land, his design was not used. But today, city designers are incorporating more of his vision by giving the entire city of Barcelona—and the entire country of Spain—a green makeover. Public transportation has increased in and around Barcelona, decreasing pollution from cars and making the air fresher.

Words to know!

emit: to send or give out something, such as smoke, gas, heat, or light.

biodiesel: fuel made from vegetable oil.

ethanol: alcohol made from plants that can be used as fuel.

TO BOOST PUBLIC TRANSPORTATION USE, SPAIN BUILT A HIGH-SPEED RAIL SYSTEM.

By 2020, an estimated 90 percent of all Spanish residents will live within 30 miles of a high-speed rail station. That will dramatically cut down on the greenhouse gases **emitted** by private cars.

What's more, Barcelona's public buses don't emit carbon dioxide. They run on electrical power, **biodiesel**, and **ethanol**.

But Barcelona didn't stop there. It also has an impressive recycling program. It's a color-coded system with recycling bins all over the city. Barcelona's local government works hard to make recycling easy for its citizens. In 2006, more than one-third of the city's total waste was **recycled**!

GREEN POWER

Sweden is another country making big changes to be greener. A leader in renewable energy, most of Sweden's electricity comes from **hydropower** and **nuclear power**. Some communities focus on using solar energy, wind power, and biofuels. Sweden set its own goal of reducing carbon dioxide emissions by 25 percent, way above the Kyoto Protocol's suggested 5 percent.

In Western Harbour, which is an urban neighborhood in the city of Malmö, Sweden, city planners designed the streets to be better for pedestrians and bicyclists. Now 40 percent of people traveling to work and 30 percent of other travelers go by bicycle!

ANOTHER COMMUNITY USES THE WORLD'S FIRST EMISSIONS-FREE ELECTRIC STREET TRAINS.

In the United States, the city of Portland, Oregon, has long been an inspiration for other cities. Portland's green transformation began in the mid-1970s when it created a waterfront park where the six-lane highway called Harbor Drive had been. The city now has more than 92,000 acres of green space, with 314 miles (505 kilometers) of biking, hiking, and running trails.

DID YOU KNOW?

The city of San Francisco, California, recycles a whopping 77 percent of its waste.

Words to know!

sustainable: designed to minimize environmental impact.

resource: anything people use to take care of themselves, such as water, food, and building materials.

As the first United States city to develop a plan to reduce greenhouse gas emissions, Portland has more than 300 **sustainable** buildings. This means they're designed to have minimal environmental impact. And about 6 percent of Portland's commuters ride their bikes to work.

ECO-CITY

More cities are focusing on how they can make their city sustainable. They can do this by both reducing their output of pollution (such as greenhouse gases, water pollution, and clogged landfills) and minimizing how much energy and other **resources** are consumed.

IT TAKES MANY DIFFERENT CHANGES TO MAKE A CITY SUSTAINABLE.

Even though people can't always agree on what the best changes are, everyone is working to create the same thing: a city that meets the needs of its current residents while protecting the environment.

As a city planner, how can you help a city become more sustainable?

Eco-industrial park: With this sustainable feature, local businesses work together to create an area where their buildings and environment are eco-friendly. Businesses in an eco-**industrial park** can share energy and water resources. They can also construct their buildings from recycled materials or materials that are environmentally friendly.

An eco-industrial park can also reduce its environmental impact with landscaping that includes native trees, grass, and flowers. They can plant trees in places where the shade will minimize the need for energy consumption such as air conditioning. Eco-industrial parks can also use renewable energy sources such as wind and solar power.

Words to know!

industrial park: a place where businesses and factories are located.

incentive: a reward that encourages someone to do something.

Transportation: For any city trying to be sustainable, transportation is a big issue. A sustainable city trying to find alternatives to buses, cars, and taxis that burn fossil fuels might add safe pedestrian and bicycle paths. Cities can also use electricity to power buses and trains. Electricity can be generated using solar, wind, or nuclear power. To encourage residents to use these alternate travel methods, cities need to make them easy to access. They can even offer **incentives** for using them.

Some residents will choose public transportation if it's cheaper than driving their cars, so minimizing costs is important. Offering low-cost bus tickets and train fares, free and safe bicycle parking, and free places to store traveling gear at work all encourage people to leave their cars at home.

Urban farming: Shipping food from faraway farms is expensive and environmentally harmful. That's why some people are finding creative ways to grow food in the city. This is called urban farming. It can be as simple as growing herbs or lettuce in a window box. Urban farming on a larger scale provides more food. Cities are supporting urban farming by giving some communities a common area where residents can plant small gardens right in the city. They can eat the produce themselves or sell it to other residents. This helps to reduce the amount of food shipped over long distances.

Urban farming also helps areas of cities called **food deserts**. These are areas that have no access to grocery stores selling fresh food. Urban farming can give residents in these areas an opportunity to make their own fresh food!

Words to know!

food desert: an area of a city with no access to fresh food.

hydroponic: growing plants in liquid, without using soil.

Urban farming doesn't have to use plots of land dedicated for growing. Roof gardens let people grow food without taking away land space below. Some people grow **hydroponically** along windowsills without any soil.

Urban infill: With this approach to sustainability, cities focus on reducing urban sprawl. Instead of pushing a city's boundaries farther into natural lands, cities find ways to use all of the available space already inside the city. To do this, cities can fix up parts of the city that have fallen to urban decay for new businesses and homes. They can also transform **historical** places into living and working spaces, even while carefully preserving their historical value.

Words to know!

historical: something used in the past.

per capita: the average of something per person.

DID YOU KNOW?

The city of Sacramento, California, claims to have more trees **per capita** than any other city. The city plans to double the number of trees between 2005 and 2045.

NATURE FIGHTS BACK

Though city buildings and roads are built to be strong, weather can still weaken them. When nature is at its most destructive, cities don't stand a chance against it.

Even a little water can cause big problems. If water seeps into the walls of a building, it eventually wears away the soft parts, causing the walls to crumble. When water freezes and expands in cold weather, it can crack water pipes under the road.

SOMETIMES NATURE IS EXTREME AND INCREDIBLY DANGEROUS. THE STRENGTH OF A CITY IS REALLY TESTED WHEN A NATURAL DISASTER HITS.

Earthquakes: Most modern cities, especially those in areas where earthquakes are common, are built to withstand movement in the earth. Minor earthquakes may cause some damage, but nothing

that can't be easily fixed. Sometimes earthquakes are more powerful—much more powerful. Trees topple and crash into buildings. Tall buildings might be okay if they're near the source of the earthquake because they can stand the up-and-down motion of the earth. But farther from the source of the earthquake, the motion of the earth is side-to-side. If strong enough, this motion can cause tall buildings to collapse.

Thick, heavy walls on shorter buildings, such as those made from bricks, can also collapse from the shaking. Buildings constructed on soft soil are more affected than buildings built on firm bedrock.

Blizzards: Huge snowstorms with blowing winds, freezing temperatures, and lots of snow can shut down a city for days. Transportation routes are closed, power goes out, and residents wait for the snowplows to make their way through the streets. City neighborhoods can be isolated for days as crews work to restore power and clear roads.

Hurricanes: In 2005, Hurricane Katrina destroyed the city of New Orleans, Louisiana. In 2012, Hurricane Sandy did major damage along the East Coast. These storms are the worst hurricanes to hit the United States in recent memory. The high winds completely destroyed small buildings. But it was the storm surges—the water that was pushed onto land by the fierce winds—that did the most dramatic damage. Entire communities were washed away or flooded for days or weeks. Even New York City's subway system was flooded, turning the tunnels into underground rivers.

While devastating, these storms have given city leaders and planners a lot of information. As cities rebuild their structures, they can make them safer for when the next storm strikes.

What are some things you as a city planner would do to rebuild a city after a natural disaster? Would you use different materials for tall buildings? Build in different areas? Construct safe places for people to stay during storms? Move buildings away from coastlines? What else might you do?

DID YOU KNOW?

Kids can contribute after a natural disaster. Hold a fundraiser at your school or collect spare change from your friends to send to humanity groups. You can hold clothing and food drives to collect items needed by families who lost their homes.

MAKE YOUR OWN
EARTHQUAKE VERSUS CITY

Although skyscrapers are built to stand through all types of weather and natural disasters, they can still collapse during earthquakes. With this project, you will see the amount of force it takes to make tall buildings fall and design types of structures that might better withstand an earthquake.

1 Sandwich the balls between the two pieces of cardboard. Use the rubber bands to hold the boards together tightly. If your rubber bands can't stretch all the way around, make a chain by looping several rubber bands together. This is your shake table. Put your shake table on a sturdy surface and cover it with the ground material.

2 Make several buildings of different sizes and shapes from your building materials. Pay attention to the materials you use. Try building an old-fashioned building that's square, with load-bearing walls. Build some modern buildings that have X-shaped cross-beams like the ones used for steel frames. Put natural landscaping in your city, such as green areas and trees.

- ☑ 2 large, stiff pieces of cardboard of equal size
- ☑ 4 balls of the same size (such as small bouncy balls or golf balls)
- ☑ large rubber bands
- ☑ building materials such as blocks, popsicle sticks, toothpicks, and clay
- ☑ ground cover materials such as sand, dirt, or rocks
- ☑ landscaping materials such as grass and small plants

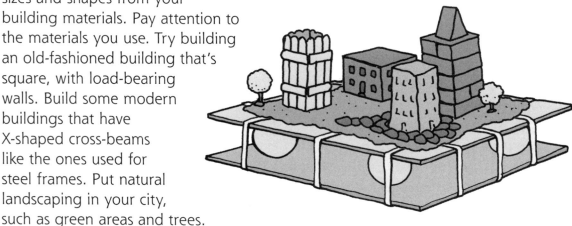

3 When you've constructed your city neighborhood, have a helper hold the bottom board steady while you gently pull the top board toward you. Let go and see what happens to your buildings.

4 Observe which buildings collapsed and which remained standing. Try to make improvements until the buildings can withstand your "earthquake."

Try This! Does the ground cover matter? Would your buildings last longer if the table were covered in a wood sheet instead of ground matter? What else could you try?

DID YOU KNOW?

When an earthquake happens under water, it pushes the water up and creates a huge wave called a tsunami that can travel great distances and even impact coastal cities. In 2011, an enormous earthquake struck off the coast of Japan. The earthquake and the tsunami it caused hit the city of Fukushima and caused horrible destruction.

MAKE YOUR OWN "GLOBAL" WARMING

With this project, you will examine how greenhouse gases affect the temperature in a city and why it's important to reduce dangerous emissions.

1 Place one thermometer in each jar. Leave one jar uncovered. Cover the second jar with plastic wrap and secure it with the rubber band.

2 Set both jars on the white paper in direct sunlight. Turn the jars so that the sunlight hits the back of the thermometers. This way, you'll be sure to get a reading of the air inside the jars.

3 The uncovered jar represents the earth with the right amount of greenhouse gases, allowing extra heat to escape from the atmosphere. The second jar represents the earth with greenhouse gases trapped in the atmosphere.

Healthy Earth

Earth with too many greenhouse gases

4 Check on the jars every 30 minutes and record the temperatures. Try to keep recording for as long as you have direct sunlight. Compare the readings on the thermometers to measure the difference between the two "atmospheres."

Try This! Put some items in the covered jar. Is the jar warmer when it's more crowded? Compare different items. How does a plant affect the temperature? How do a few stacks of coins affect the temperature? Make sure you do the experiments with the same amount of direct sunlight.

DID YOU KNOW?

To improve its sustainability, Paris, France, uses sheep to mow the grassy areas around the city!

MAKE YOUR OWN
FUTURE CITY

SUPPLIES

☑ poster board or large paper
☑ markers

Though new cities aren't often built anymore, current cities are always growing and changing to improve life for their residents. Cities such as Portland, Oregon, have even reversed development, like turning a highway into a greenway! With this project, you will design your own city of the future.

1 What will cities of the future will be like? There will definitely be a lot of people! Most people on earth already live in cities, and urban populations will continue to grow faster than rural populations.

2 Draw your future city on your poster board. Include all the parts of a city you've learned about and use all your city-planning knowledge. Incorporate today's real sustainable features plus the ones you've invented. Consider the practical parts of your future city, like how people will commute in eco-friendly ways and how they'll get their food locally. What does your ideal sustainable city look like?

Try This! Is your future city near an ocean or a desert? In the mountains or a valley? How does the natural geography of the land affect your city's layout? Are there different safety needs because of where your city is built?

GRAFFITI

Graffiti is a big part of many urban landscapes—people illegally paint on building walls, subway cars, roads, and sidewalks. Some people say graffiti is an art form and others say it's destruction of property. Banksy is a famous artist from Great Britain whose graffiti has become very popular with both city residents and art collectors.

MAKE YOUR OWN
HYDROPONIC PLANTER

Growing plants is a great way to make cities more sustainable. Since land and nutrient-rich soil is not readily available in cities, hydroponics is becoming popular in urban spaces. Make your own basic hydroponic planter and experiment with alternative planting materials.

1 Cut the 2-liter bottle in half, leaving the cap on. Make a hole in the cap big enough to fit your material strip through. Thread it through, making sure it's long enough to have some material in the top of the bottle and some material resting in the bottom of the bottle.

2 Fill the bottom half of the bottle with water. Follow the directions on the litmus paper to measure the pH of your water. Plants need a pH 5–7 to grow well. If your water isn't in this range, add lemon juice to lower the pH or a teaspoon of baking soda to increase it. When the pH is right, add plant nutrients to the water using the instructions on the container.

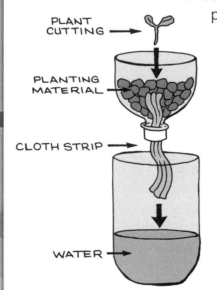

PLANT CUTTING →

PLANTING MATERIAL →

CLOTH STRIP →

WATER →

3 Turn the bottle top upside down with the fabric still in place and fill it with your planting material. Tuck your plant runner in the middle of this material. Make sure your fabric reaches both the top and bottom halves so it can transport water up to the plant.

4 Set the top half of the bottle onto the bottom half. Make sure that the water is moving up the fabric to the plant. You'll need to change the water once a week, repeating Step 2 each time.

5 Once your plant's roots get bigger, you can take the cap off and remove the fabric. This will allow the roots to reach down into the water. You'll need to add oxygen to the water to prevent the roots from getting slimy. Cut a piece of aquarium tubing long enough to run down through the hole in the bottle top. Use a small air pump or a hollow rubber ball with the tubing poked into it. You'll need to pump the ball once a day to add oxygen to the water.

Try This! Make more hydroponic planters with different plants and different planting materials. Are there certain plants that thrive with hydroponics? Are there certain planting materials that better support plant growth? Keep experimenting until you have just the right hydroponic planter!

URBAN ANIMALS

Although many animals have been pushed out of their **habitat** by urban development, there are some critters that have adapted to cities.

Words to know!

habitat: the natural area where a plant or animal lives.

The most common city animal is the pigeon. These birds have plenty of food and water in the city, very few natural predators, and plenty of places to roost. Many residents are annoyed with pigeons because pigeon droppings coat many surfaces and can cause diseases in people, in addition to damaging buildings, cars, and monuments.

Pigeons aren't the only birds to call cities home. Crows, blue jays, owls, and even falcons live in cities. Over time, other animals have found that cities provide food and shelter. Raccoons and squirrels and even larger animals such as coyotes and red foxes have begun to live in cities. City coyotes are growing more skilled at finding food and avoiding detection.

In Africa and India, monkeys have moved into urban areas. They boldly approach open food markets and enter homes looking for food.

CHAPTER 10
Each City Is Unique

What makes each city different from every other city? When you think of Los Angeles, California, what do you think sets it apart from other cities? Do you think of Hollywood? Orlando, Florida, has Disney World. Paris, France, has beautiful landmarks such as the Eiffel Tower. Every major city has its own distinct personality and landmarks. Cities are known for all kinds of **characteristics**, such as Chicago's deep-dish pizza, Boston's Fenway Park, and London's double-decker buses in England.

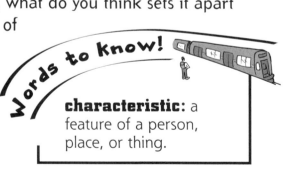

Words to know!

characteristic: a feature of a person, place, or thing.

How do these unique personalities and characteristics develop? How does each city become different from the rest? A city's characteristics are affected by lots of things, such as location and landscape and what kind of attractions it offers. Cities usually have a mix of historical attractions and places built just to bring visitors.

CASHING IN

Some cities are **financial** centers. New York, London, and Tokyo are the three biggest, followed by Hong Kong, Singapore, and Chicago. To be a financial center, a city has to have a lot of banks, businesses, and **stock exchanges** that reach the **global** community. The city also has to have access to a lot of money and a good legal system to control where the money goes.

Wall Street in New York City, home to the New York Stock Exchange, is the oldest and most famous financial center. In Colonial America, Wall Street was built with an earthen wall along it for protection. A huge sycamore tree, called a buttonwood tree at the time, was a gathering place there for traders to make deals. In 1792, these traders made an agreement called the Buttonwood Agreement that said the participants of trades would deal only with each other. This agreement was the beginning of the New York Stock Exchange.

Soon after traders entered into the Buttonwood Agreement, the Erie Canal was built. The canal connected the inland Great Lakes to the East Coast through New York City. As trade through New York increased, Wall Street became the "money capital of America."

During the Civil War in the 1860s, the South struggled economically while the North became wealthier. New York City became a major banking center, connecting money in Europe with financial growth in North America. In modern times, Wall Street continues to play a major role in the world's financial community.

KEEP AUSTIN WEIRD

While some cities take themselves very seriously, others embrace how strange they are. The slogan of Austin, Texas, is "Keep Austin Weird."

The slogan was created to bring visitors to Austin, and it was soon supported by residents who love the idea that their city is especially unique. Residents claim that their city is the "live music capital of the world." Since 1987, Austin has hosted an annual music and film festival called South By Southwest, which is one of the most respected festivals of its kind.

Austin is also home to a bat colony of 1.5 million bats that live under a bridge. To the delight of visitors and residents, the bats come swooping out each evening.

Austin isn't the only city known for its quirks. New Orleans' jazz scene and unique food draw people there all year long. Burlington, Vermont, is home to hipster Ben & Jerry's ice cream and is a place people visit to experience interesting, locally sourced restaurants and unusual art galleries.

DID YOU KNOW?

New York may be famous for Wall Street, but people visit the city to walk through Times Square, see a Broadway show, tour the Statue of Liberty, or explore the American Museum of Natural History or the Museum of Modern Art. These are just a few of New York's many attractions.

BARELY RECOGNIZE YOU!

Sometimes a city is known for things that don't attract visitors. Then those who advertise for the city have to work hard to make their city known for attractive things. When people think about Buffalo, New York, the first thing they might think about is bad weather and disappointing sports teams. Neither of these characteristics gives anyone much of a reason to visit Buffalo.

Advertisers, politicians, sports teams, and other businesses in Buffalo worked together on a new slogan for the city. They came up with "Buffalo. For Real." Their goal was to take the focus away from massive snowdrifts and disappointing sports teams. The new promotions showed scenes of historic western New York that showcase the history and beauty of Buffalo.

Cities have to work hard to change negative perceptions. When tourists come to a city, they spend money in the city, which helps local businesses thrive. If some of these visitors really like the city and decide to move there, it helps the city grow.

CITY LANDMARKS AND PERSONALITIES

Many cities have landmarks that attract visitors, such as the National Mall and Washington Monument in Washington, DC. Landmarks are buildings or structures that are unique to each city. Some landmarks have been in their city for hundreds of years. But new landmarks may be instantly popular. **Below are six cities and their landmarks.**

Leaning Tower of Pisa in Pisa, Italy: The builders of the tower didn't mean to make it lean! Construction started in the year 1173 and continued for hundreds of years. The building started to lean because the foundation was set into soft soil that began to sink almost immediately. For nearly 100 years, construction stopped and the soil settled. When construction resumed, engineers made the upper floors with one side taller than the other to keep the building from toppling completely.

Words to know!

symbol: something that stands for or represents something else.

Statue of Liberty in New York City, New York: The statue was a gift of friendship from the people of France to New York, dedicated as a **symbol** of freedom and democracy in 1886. The statue was shipped in parts to the United States, where it was reassembled at the entrance to New York Harbor.

DID YOU KNOW?

The Eiffel Tower isn't the only famous landmark in Paris. There's also a 40-foot-high statue of a thumb called "Le Pouce," which is French for "the thumb."

Sydney Opera House in Sydney, Australia: This modern building opened in 1973. With its arching shell design, it is now one of the busiest performing arts centers in the world. More than 3,000 events are attended each year by more than 2 million people.

Forbidden City in Beijing, China: Built in the early 1400s, this was the imperial palace for almost 500 years, the center of Chinese government, and where the emperors lived. Now the Forbidden City is a major tourist attraction and museum.

Elizabeth Tower of the Palace of Westminster in London, England: This famous clock tower was built in 1859 and houses the large bell affectionately named "Big Ben." At 316 feet (96 meters) tall, it is the third-tallest free-standing clock tower and one of the most popular landmarks in London.

Words to know!

calligraphy: beautiful writing or fancy lettering.

Taj Mahal in Agra, India: This white-domed marble structure was built in the 1630s and 1640s by an emperor as a tribute to his wife. The Taj Mahal is filled with gardens, reflecting pools, **calligraphy**, and other beautiful details.

MAKE YOUR OWN
REGIONAL RECIPES

Some cities are known for certain foods that tourists come to eat. Here's your chance to try some popular, regional recipes. **Caution: You will be using a knife and the stove, so have an adult help with this project.**

BUFFALO WINGS

There are different stories about the origin of Buffalo wings, but the end result is the same—fried chicken wings in a spicy sauce. Even though they're usually fried, you can bake them at home. **Ingredients:** *chicken wings, 1 tablespoon vegetable oil, 1 teaspoon salt, 1 cup all-purpose flour, 6 tablespoons hot sauce, 6 tablespoons unsalted butter or margarine, celery sticks, blue cheese dressing*

1 Preheat the oven to 425 degrees Fahrenheit (232 degrees Celsius). Line a baking sheet with aluminum foil and coat it with cooking spray.

2 Have an adult cut whole wings into two pieces. Toss the wings with the oil and salt.

3 Put the flour in a plastic bag, add the wings, seal it closed, and shake them until the wings are covered in flour.

4 Remove the wings, shake off the excess flour, and spread them out on the foil-lined baking pan. Bake for 20 minutes, then have an adult help you turn the wings over. Cook another 20 minutes or until the wings are cooked through.

5 While the wings are baking, melt the butter and mix it with the hot sauce. This is your Buffalo sauce.

6 After the wings are cooked, put them in a large mixing bowl. Pour the Buffalo sauce over the hot wings and toss to completely coat. Serve with celery sticks and blue cheese dressing.

BALTIMORE CRAB CAKES

Coastal Virginia and Maryland are known for crab cakes. These tasty cakes are usually served with coleslaw. **Ingredients:** *½ teaspoon Old Bay seasoning, 1 egg, 1 teaspoon Worcestershire sauce, ⅛ teaspoon dry mustard, 1 tablespoon mayonnaise, ½ teaspoon lemon juice, 1½ teaspoons mustard, 1½ teaspoons melted butter, ½ teaspoon parsley flakes, ¼ cup breadcrumbs, 8 ounces fresh crabmeat*

1 In a large mixing bowl, combine all the ingredients except for the crabmeat. Gently fold in the crabmeat, being careful not to break up the lumps too much.

2 Shape the mixture into small cakes with your hands, pressing them firmly together. Press them well onto a greased cookie sheet. Refrigerate for an hour.

3 Bake your crab cakes at 375 degrees Fahrenheit (190 degrees Celsius) until evenly brown, 12 to 15 minutes. The internal temperature should be 165 degrees Fahrenheit (74 degrees Celsius). Serve hot with coleslaw and enjoy!

COBB SALAD

This California-based salad is hearty enough to serve as a whole meal by itself! **Ingredients:** *2 slices cooked bacon, ¼ head romaine lettuce, torn into bite-size pieces, 1 hard-boiled egg, peeled and chopped, 1 cup diced cooked chicken, ½ avocado, peeled and diced, ½ tomato, chopped, 1 ounce Roquefort cheese, crumbled, ⅛ teaspoon Dijon mustard, 1 tablespoon red wine vinegar, ¼ teaspoon Worcestershire sauce, ½ clove crushed garlic, pinch of salt, pinch of ground black pepper, 2 tablespoons olive oil*

1 Whisk together the mustard, vinegar, Worcestershire sauce, garlic, salt, and pepper. Slowly drizzle in the olive oil while whisking constantly to form the dressing.

2 Put the lettuce on your plate and arrange the egg, bacon (crumbled), chicken, avocado, tomato, and cheese on top of the lettuce. Drizzle the dressing evenly over the salad and serve immediately.

MAKE YOUR OWN CITY LANDMARK

SUPPLIES

☑ building materials such as plaster of Paris, clay, drawing paper, wood, cardboard, paper tubes

Even if you live in a city that already has a famous landmark, it's fun to brainstorm another one. If you live in a city or town without a landmark, make up one that would fit the place you live. Who knows—your design might catch everyone's interest and become an actual landmark some day!

1 Spend some time thinking about your town. What do you like about it? What do you dislike about it? Why do people come to visit your town? What do visitors like the most? Has your town ever been famous for something? Does it have a special food, type of music, or unique sport?

Words to know!

replica: a copy of an object.

2 Use your imagination to think of a landmark that can symbolize what is special about your town. The Statue of Liberty symbolizes freedom and democracy. Landmarks are more than just a **replica** of something.

3 Use your materials to construct a small version of your landmark.

Try This! Measure your landmark and use those proportions to figure out how big it should be in real life. Then figure out the best place for your landmark in your town or city.

adapt: changes a person, plant, or animal makes to survive.

alphabetically: in order by letter—a, b, c, etc.

alternating current (AC): electricity that flows back and forth at a steady rate.

antenna: a metal rod on a building used to receive radio or television signals.

aqueduct: a channel that transports water from its source over a great distance.

asphalt: a black tar that is used to pave roads.

atmosphere: the blanket of air surrounding the earth.

automated: controlled by a computer instead of by a person.

BCE: put after a date, BCE stands for Before Common Era and counts down to zero. CE stands for Common Era and counts up from zero. These non-religious terms correspond to BC and AD.

bedrock: the solid rock earth, well beneath the softer surface of soil, sand, clay, gravel, or water.

biodiesel: fuel made from vegetable oil.

biological: anything that is or was living.

calligraphy: beautiful writing or fancy lettering.

canal: a man-made channel used to deliver water.

carbon monoxide: a poisonous gas produced by burning fossil fuels such as gasoline.

Census Bureau: the department in the United States government that every 10 years takes the census, which is an official count of all the people living in an area.

chamber pot: a large, bowl-shaped pot used as an indoor toilet.

characteristic: a feature of a person, place, or thing.

commerce: the activity of buying, selling, and trading.

community: all the people living in a particular area or place.

commuters: the people who go to work every morning and then home every evening during the week.

concrete: a hard construction material made with cement, sand, and water.

contaminant: any pollutant or object that could harm a living organism.

conveyor: a moving belt that carries objects from one place to another.

council: a group of elected officials.

crop: a plant grown for food or other uses.

culture: the beliefs and way of life of a group of people.

debris: the scattered pieces of something that has been broken or destroyed.

decay: to rot.

direct current (DC): electricity that flows in one direction.

efficient: making the most of time and energy.

element: a substance that cannot be broken down into a simpler substance, such as oxygen and gold. Everything is made up of combinations of elements.

emit: to send or give out something, such as smoke, gas, heat, or light.

engineer: someone who designs or builds things such as roads, bridges, and buildings.

environment: everything in nature, living and nonliving, including animals, plants, rocks, soil, and water.

established: a custom, belief, practice, or place that is recognized after having been in existence for a long enough time.

ethanol: alcohol made from plants that can be used as fuel.

excavation: making a trench or tunnel by digging.

extinguish: to put out.

factory: a large place where goods are made.

federal: the national government of a country.

financial: having to do with money.

fire escape: a metal stairway on the outside of a building to use to escape a fire.

food desert: an area of a city with no access to fresh food.

food stamps: the common name for a program officially called the Supplemental Nutrition Assistance Program. This government program gives low-income people a debit card they can use in stores to buy food.

fossil: the remains or traces of ancient plants or animals.

fossil fuels: oil, natural gas, and coal, which are natural fuels that formed long ago from the remains of living organisms.

generator: a machine that converts mechanical energy into electricity.

global: relating to the entire world.

global warming: an increase in the average temperature of the earth's atmosphere, enough to cause climate change.

goods: items that can be bought, sold, or traded.

greenhouse gas: a gas such as water vapor, carbon dioxide, or methane that traps heat and contributes to warming temperatures.

habitat: the natural area where a plant or animal lives.

historical: something used in the past.

hydroponic: growing plants in liquid, without using soil.

hydropower: using flowing water to create energy.

immigrate: to move from one country to live in another.

incentive: a reward that encourages someone to do something.

industrial park: a place where businesses and factories are located.

Industrial Revolution: a time of far-reaching change when the large-scale production of goods began.

infrared: a kind of image that shows how hot (or cool) its subject is.

infrastructure: the large-scale public systems, services, and facilities of a country or region, including power and water supplies, public transportation, telecommunications, roads, and schools.

irrigation: a system of transporting water through canals or tunnels to water crops.

Kyoto Protocol: the international agreement to reduce greenhouse gases around the world.

landscape: a large area of land with specific features.

latrine: a bathroom that can be used by several people at once, often as simple as a long trench dug in the earth.

livestock: animals raised for food and other uses.

load-bearing: supporting the bulk of the weight of a structure.

manhole: a round opening that provides access below a street.

manufacturing industry: the production of large quantities of products, usually in a factory.

mayor: the elected official in charge of a city's government.

mechanical: done by machine, not by a person.

metropolitan: describes a city and its surrounding area.

microfiltration: to filter something using extremely fine filters.

microorganism: a living thing that is so tiny it can only be seen using a microscope. Bacteria, fungi, and algae are all microorganisms.

migrate: to move from one place to another when seasons change.

migration: the movement of a large group of animals or people from one location to another.

municipal: having to do with a city's activities or management.

nomad: a person who moves from place to place in search of food.

nuclear power: power produced by splitting atoms.

numerically: in order by number—1, 2, 3, etc.

organic: something that is or was living, such as wood, paper, grass, and insects.

origin: the place or moment when something comes into existence.

outhouse: an outdoor toilet built over a hole in the ground.

pedestrian: someone traveling on foot.

per capita: the average of something per person.

plumbing: the pipes that carry water in and out of a building.

pollutant: waste material that damages the environment.

population: all of the people in an area or in a group.

postindustrial: describes an area formerly used for manufacturing.

power grid: a network of cables above and below ground that carries electrical power throughout a region.

pressure: a force that pushes on an object.

public transportation: transportation such as buses and trains that anyone can use by paying a fare.

pump: a device that moves water or other liquids.

rapid transit: a transportation system that moves a lot of people around a city quickly and smoothly.

recycle: shredding, squashing, pulping, or melting items to use the materials to create new products.

reduce: to use less of something.

renewable energy: energy that doesn't get used up, including solar and wind.

replica: a copy of an object.

reservoir: a manmade or natural lake used to collect water that can be stored for future use.

resident: a person living in a particular place.

resource: anything people use to take care of themselves, such as water, food, and building materials.

rural: relating to the countryside rather than a city or town.

service: work done for others as a job or business, such as a doctor providing medical services.

sewer: a drain for wastewater.

sinkhole: a hole or depression in the land that opens up suddenly.

society: an organized community of people.

spire: a pointy structure that decorates the top of a building.

steam powered: powered by an engine that burns wood or coal to heat water and create steam.

stock exchange: a place where people trade shares of businesses.

story: a floor in a building.

stress: pressure or strain caused by a large amount of weight.

sub-Saharan Africa: the part of Africa that is south of the Sahara Desert.

suburban: relating to an outlying district of a city.

subway: an underground railroad, especially one powered by electricity.

sustainable: designed to minimize environmental impact.

symbol: something that stands for or represents something else.

synchronized: working together in a pattern.

tenement: a multi-family living space, usually occupied by poor people.

third rail: the source of power for electric subway systems; a brush, wheel, or sliding "shoe" touches the rail and sends power to the train's electric motor.

tourist: a traveler who visits a place for fun.

track geometry car: the vehicle that runs on subway systems to monitor the conditions of the system and report if anything needs to be fixed or repaired.

trading center: a central place where people meet to exchange goods.

transformer: a device that changes the voltage of electricity.

treatment plant: where wastewater is sent through a cleaning process.

trolley: a large cart.

tunnel: an underground passageway that goes through or under natural or manmade obstacles such as rivers, mountains, roads, and buildings.

Twitter: an online service that allows users to send and read messages called tweets. Tweets are limited to 140 characters. undeveloped: not built on or changed.

unique: special or unusual.

unsanitary: something that is dirty and unhealthy.

urban: relating to a city or large town.

urban decay: when a city or part of a city is neglected or virtually abandoned.

urban heat island: a dense cityscape that raises the temperature in the surrounding area.

urban renewal: the development of urban areas that have become run down, by renovating old buildings or building new ones.

vegetation: all the plant life in a particular area.

ventilation shaft: a tunnel or passage that brings in fresh air.

veto: to reject a law or policy.

voltage: the force that moves electricity along a wire.

wastewater: water that has been used by people in their homes, in factories, and in other businesses and is now dirty.

wildlife: animals, birds, and other things that live wild in nature.

xeriscaping: landscaping with rocks and plants that need very little or no water.

BOOkS

The Human World (The World in Infographics),
Jon Richards, Owlkids Books, October 2013.

Urban Habitats (Discovery Education: Habitats), Kate
Mcallan, Powerkids Press, July 2013.

Ancient Cities (Discovery Education: Ancient Civilizations),
Louise Park, Powerkids Press, January 2013.

*New York City History for Kids: From New Amsterdam to the Big Apple with
21 Activities,* Richard Panchyk, Chicago Review Press, November 2012.

Potatoes on Rooftops: Farming in the City, Hadley Dyer, Annick Press, July 2012.

Just Add Water: Making the City of Chicago,
Renee Kreczmer, Lake Claremont Press, June 2012.

WEB SITES

Video on Accessible Pedestrian Signals
www.youtube.com/watch?v=ALFrGaWXMqQ

Kids and Community
www.planning.org/kidsandcommunity

PBS Building Big
www.pbs.org/wgbh/buildingbig

Skyscrapers
www.skyscraper.org

Recycle City
www.epa.gov/recyclecity

US Government Site for Kids
kids.usa.gov

Midtown Manhattan Growth Animation
www.youtube.com/watch?v=NULrNgCVbT8

Youth for Public Transport
y4pt.org